SMART MONEY

Education and Economic Development

William Schweke

ECONOMIC POLICY INSTITUTE

About the Author

William Schweke is the research director for the Corporation for Enterprise Development (CFED); he is based in the organization's Durham, N.C. office. CFED is a nonprofit organization that creates economic opportunity by helping the poor save, invest, succeed as entrepreneurs, and participate as contributors to and beneficiaries of the economy. The organization identifies and researches promising ideas, collaborates with the public and private sectors to test them, and helps drive the application and adoption of proven concepts. Established in 1979, CFED works nationally and internationally through its offices in Washington D.C., Durham, and San Francisco.

Acknowledgments

The author would like to thank Tracy Constantine, Jessica Treat, and Beadsie Woo for editorial feedback, a bit of writing and research, and copy editing help.

This project is part of
the EPI Education Research Program

ECONOMIC POLICY INSTITUTE
1660 L Street, NW, Suite 1200
Washington, D.C. 20036

http://www.epinet.org

ISBN: 1-932066-10-1

Table of contents

Executive summary

Strong economies compete on the basis of high value, not solely low cost. Yet in the United States, growing economic disparity hinders the nation's ability to provide the high-value-added products and services necessary to compete in a global marketplace. The economic problems associated with unequal growth – stagnant wage growth and depressed market demand – in turn exacerbate social problems, such as crime, drug abuse, gangs, reliance on transfer payments, and family break-ups.

The most forward-thinking approach to solving these problems and increasing competitiveness is to equip today's and tomorrow's citizens with the skills and attitudes for economic and civic success in an increasingly knowledge-based economy. Yet education funding has been losing ground over the past several years, at a time when the knowledge-based economy demands an increasingly higher set of skills and when growing numbers of public school students are minorities or new immigrants.

A compelling body of research links primary and secondary education to economic development and growth. This research recognizes people as a type of economic asset – "human capital" – and shows that increased investment in health, skills, and knowledge provides future returns to the economy through increases in labor productivity. Education increases workers' average earnings and productivity, and it also reduces the incidence of social problems such as drug abuse, crime, welfare dependency, and lack of access to medical care, all of which can weigh heavily on the economy.

Research confirms the value of investing in educational programs, curricula, technologies, skills, and infrastructure, particularly in the areas of:

Pre-school. Longitudinal studies calculate a significant return on investment for preschool education as well as net public-dollar savings due to the decreased likelihood for preschool participants to repeat grades, require remedial education, be incarcerated for crimes, and become dependent on welfare. Many states are moving toward offering subsidized preschool, particularly for at-risk children, but funding these programs remains a challenge.

Primary and secondary education. Research shows that a high-quality education increases the earnings of individuals and the economic health of their communities. Some believe, however, that increased public investment will not necessarily improve the quality of education offered. But recent studies show that education spending can have a direct, positive impact on the business climate and can improve the success of at-risk students, whose contributions to the economy are critical for achieving a high-value/high-wage economy in the 21st century. Such spending will have a greater chance of success if coupled with specific reforms, such as smaller class sizes, greater access to technology for at-risk students, support for teacher training and innovation, and improved accountability structures.

Community colleges. The rate of return on community college education is positive; those who attend community college earn significantly higher wages than those who stop at a high school diploma. Because of their low cost and lack of requirements for admission, community colleges have become the postsecondary organizations that many disadvantaged groups use to gain access to employment. Thus, community colleges are well-positioned to help bridge the educational, wage, race, and class divides in America.

Supporting this continuum of programs will require a financial commitment. Given the significant return on investment that a productive education and training infrastructure can bring, federal and state governments need to take a leading role and a long-term perspective. Such a long-term and forward-thinking perspective demands courageous reform of the current tax system. Specifically, states and localities need to consider these strategies:

- curb the use of business incentive programs, which give businesses economic breaks but do not guarantee local job creation or economic growth;

- halt the use of corporate tax-sheltering loopholes, which are eroding revenues generated by state corporate income taxes;

- modernize state and local revenue systems to be more efficient, effective, customer-friendly, and accountable.

If the United States is to achieve a higher and more shared standard of living, U.S. firms must compete on the basis of new, higher-quality service and production approaches that utilize new technologies and a more skilled workforce. Economic developers call this the "high road." Taking the high road will require that the nation develop a more seamless, well-endowed lifelong learning system; reform wasteful business incentive programs and redirect the resulting savings into education or other state priorities; and create and maintain a modernized, high-quality revenue system.

States and localities must find ways to encourage more of their employment in high-value sectors and workplaces. A high-quality education and training continuum, while not alone sufficient, is a necessary condition for meeting this challenge.

Introduction

Strong economies compete on the basis of high value, not solely low cost. A nation or a state that offers a skilled labor force, modern infrastructure, and a high quality of life, yet has relatively higher taxes, can hardly be called anti-business. Yet in the United States, where inequality in earnings and wealth has been increasing for two decades, growing economic disparity is hindering the nation's ability to provide the high-value-added products and services necessary to compete in a global marketplace. And as wages for working people stagnate, families struggle to make ends meet, and market demand falls. Economic problems, in turn, exacerbate social problems, such as crime, drug abuse, gangs, reliance on government assistance, and family break-ups. To ameliorate these weaknesses in the social fabric, public funds that might otherwise go toward productive investment are spent instead on crime control, drug treatment, and income support programs.

Prevention is almost always cheaper than treatment. If we do not invest now, we most certainly will pay later.

The most forward-thinking approach to solving these problems and increasing U.S. competitiveness is to equip today's and tomorrow's citizens with the skills and attitudes for economic and civic success in an increasingly knowledge-based economy. There is a growing consensus that money spent wisely on education pays off not only for workers but also for communities and businesses. Educational attainment raises incomes and increases productivity, while failures in educating the workforce are associated with higher levels of crime and welfare dependency.

Today American states and elected officials are faced with fiscal crises that sometimes lead them to cut the funding streams for these public services. Over the long haul, however, states will position themselves better if they develop practical, long-term plans for sustained investments in education, workforce preparation, and retraining. A key element of these plans must be increased accountability in school spending, reform of the tax systems that finance education, and reform of business tax incentive programs that siphon away revenue for no productive purpose.

Investing wisely in education generates real, quantifiable results for workers, businesses, and society. If people are tied to low-paying jobs and unable to acquire skills needed by employers, productivity grows more slowly. If businesses do not have a workforce that is appropriately educated, they will be less competitive with their overseas rivals. If citizens do not have what it takes to succeed in today's economy, they will feel threatened by economic change and are much more likely to recycle back and forth between unemployment insurance, welfare, and poorly paid, insecure employment. Finally, the spreading number of low-paying jobs breaks a longstanding social contract under which most people work: "If I work hard, I will be able to keep my job, support my family, and enjoy a growing income." Quality education is a critical tool for upholding this implicit contract.

CHAPTER 1

What is economic development?

At its most basic, economic development is the process by which wealth is created, or the way in which a society increases its level of material and social well-being over time. In a developing economy, employment increases, incomes rise, innovation occurs, and productivity grows.

Economic development should be concerned with how all people fare in the development process, regardless of wealth, educational status, or ethnicity. It should help to achieve a more widely shared and sustainable standard of living. This overall goal has roughly three elements:

- *Development* entails the enrichment of material and social well-being. It can be measured in the flow of money and goods to individuals over time; increases in the quality and quantity of public goods (such as clean air and water, freedom from fear of crime, better schools, etc.); and access to good jobs with wages and benefits sufficient for supporting a family, and opportunities for advancement).
- *Shared growth* means that there is broad distribution of opportunities for meaningful participation in the economy and enjoyment of the benefits of an increased standard of living.
- *Sustained prosperity* means that the above goals are achieved in a manner that does not detract from — but rather enhances — the economy's ability to achieve the same goals in the future.

In the global economy, competitive advantage is based increasingly on the education and skills of the labor force. States and communities must make wise investments in public education in order to create a positive business climate. But fulfilling this priority does not mean simply throwing more money at education. Rather, it means moving dollars from low-yield economic development programs, such as business tax incentives, and getting the most value out of education spending. Schools need to adapt to a changing world and changing technologies, be more accountable for student outcomes, and help in forming closer ties between the worlds of school and work. Businesses, on the other hand, need to modernize so that they will create a demand for students with higher skills.

CHAPTER 2

Why investment in education matters

Judging by the growing number of school-business partnerships at the local level and the participation of corporate leaders in education policy discussions at all levels of government, it seems that business leaders generally place a great deal of value on education. Unlike taxes and regulation, education is not usually the primary target of those bent on cutting budgets and shrinking the role of government in an effort to promote a "good business climate."

Yet, as with all public expenditures, education has to compete for scarce resources with other uses of public funds. Indeed, while K-12 still accounts for one of the largest shares of state general fund appropriations and while such spending has grown in real terms up until 2002, education funding has been losing ground to other expenditures for the past several years. During that time, Medicaid has been the fastest-growing expenditure in most states.[1]

This dwindling proportion of investment in education comes at a time when the knowledge-based U.S. economy demands an increasingly higher set of skills that school will have to provide, and at a time when increasing numbers of public school students are minorities or new immigrants. Unless the rising proportion of economically disadvantaged pupils in U.S. schools enters the workforce with skills in proportion to those of their more affluent peers, the United States will not be able to operate at the level of workforce skill necessary for a successful high-wage, global economy.

The following section expands on these issues by looking more closely at specific links between primary and secondary education and economic development.[2]

Does education contribute to economic development?

Over the past several decades, beginning with the path-breaking work of Nobel laureate Theodore W. Schultz,[3] economists and business leaders alike have come to recognize the contribution of the skills and knowledge of the labor force to long-term economic growth. Rather than seeing people simply as one of three interchangeable factors of production (land, labor, and capital), human capital theory argues that people are the "moving part" in economic development. Without them, technologies would not be invented, land would not be cultivated, production lines would not be staffed, and capital would not be invested. People are also a type of economic asset for which increased investment in health, skills, and knowledge provides future returns to the economy through increases in labor productivity.

Numerous studies have quantified the contribution of education (through its impact on human capital formation) to total economic growth. In reviewing these, Roland Sturm of the Rand Corporation concludes that "regardless of the particular calculation, education and its effect through labor quality are generally found to be among the most important contributors to economic growth" (Sturm 1993). Brookings Institution scholar Edward Denison attributes 14% of the nation's economic growth between 1929 and 1982 to improvements in education, and 27% to higher levels of education among those employed (Denison 1985). Research by economist Eric Hanushek (an economist who, as we will discuss below, is one of the leading skeptics about the value of increased school spending) and Dongwook Kim (1995) shows that economies in countries with higher international test scores in mathematics and science grow faster than those with lower scores.

Moreover, education's contribution to economic growth seems to be increasing over time. Due to rapid advances in technology, ideas are increasingly being substituted for physical matter in the creation of economic value.[4] In this environment, enterprises that add value by increasing the "conceptual content of output" are the ones that generate higher returns for owners and pay higher wages to workers. Thus, a high-quality educational system to train "knowledge workers" is a prerequisite for a high-value economy. While creating such a system does not guarantee a shift toward higher-value activity, without top-level schools a community is unlikely to achieve a high-value/high-wage economy.

Human capital theory has helped focus attention on the role labor skills play in economic growth, yet recent theories of economic development take an even more comprehensive view of the impact of human input on economic growth. For example, based on evidence that the birth of new firms and the growth of existing firms have a significant impact on economic progress, economic development theorists have increasingly recognized the role that entrepreneurial activity plays in economic growth.[5] Other development theorists have explored the importance of knowledge and technology in regional economic development.[6]

Around the globe, education has long been recognized as one of the wisest investments in individual economic success. In a review of literature on returns to education across 44 countries, World Bank economist George Psacharopoulos (1981) calculates "internal rates of return" to education of 14% and 12% for secondary and higher education, respectively, in developed countries.[7] A recent unpublished study by Christofides, Behr, and Neelakantan finds that the income gap between urban and rural counties in Pennsylvania can be attributed to the educational gap between those counties.

Among the numerous studies of factors that influence aggregate economic growth, four notable studies include an education spending variable.

Timothy Bartik of the W. E. Upjohn Institute for Employment Research concludes that spending on state and local public services, including primary, secondary, and higher education, can have a positive impact on private sector productivity and output (Bartik 1996). In an extraordinary example of the benefits of public investment, Bartik finds that "a property-tax-financed increase in higher education spending of one percent of a state's personal income would increase state manufacturing output in the long run by 8.3%" (Bartik 1996, 20). Yet, most of the findings from this study show rather modest effects of public services expenditures on economic growth. As a result, Bartik concludes that "an increase in taxes, if used to finance an increase in public-services spending, is unlikely to have *significant negative* effects upon a state's economic development" (Bartik 1996, 32) The implication, in Bartik's words, is that "states can make fiscal policy decisions without fear of the economic development consequences" (Bartik 1996, 32).

These findings are roughly backed up by earlier and later studies. In a report on the effects of a series of business climate variables on employment growth in the 48 states between 1973 and 1980, Michael Wasylenko found a significant positive relationship between education spending and total employment growth.[8] Wasylenko's research indicated that a 1% increase in spending on education relative to income was associated with a 0.72% increase in total employment over the period. Based on these findings, Wasylenko concluded that "higher expenditure on education relative to income has positive effects on overall employment growth, and budget-cutters should not reduce education expenditures very much, if at all" (Wasylenko 1986).

Moreover, in a comprehensive review of the literature on public expenditures and the states for the Federal Reserve Bank of Boston, Ronald Fisher notes that the sheer variety of conceptual and measurement issues that characterize these studies make it difficult to determine the importance of public services in business location decisions. Taking a more conditional view, Fisher states that at least "*some* public services clearly have a positive effect on *some* measures of economic development in *some* cases" (Bradbury et al. 1997, 4). Transportation services show the strongest link, then public safety, and then education. Yet he also suggests that some of the positive effects of education spending are not captured in these studies, because the benefits spread to other jurisdictions and the nation over time. So, weaker local effects of educational investment might translate into stronger national effects over time (Fisher 1997).

Hungerford and Wassmer have conducted one of the best recent reviews of this literature and made a clear contribution by distilling the key criteria of a good study on this topic. They summarize five discrete studies that present "balance budget" analyses of the impact of additional K-12 public spending on development indicators. (The balance budget criterion means any increase in spending would entail a tax increase, and any cut in taxes would lead to cuts in public services.) They state:

> It is quite clear from our review of five different regression studies that attempt to measure the influence of public spending on primary and secondary education on economic development in the United States that this category of government expenditure exerts a measurable and statistically significant influence on it. Recall that this positive influence has been calculated by simulating an increase in per-pupil expenditure that is funded by either raising a miscellaneous tax or fee, or cutting public expenditures on transfer

> payments. The study by Helms even shows that financing an increase in public K-12 education expenditure by any means except a state budget deficit or by cutting public expenditures on health or higher education will lead to both short- and long-run increases in a state's personal income. (Hungerford and Wassmer 2003, 47)

Education and earnings

Spending on education contributes to community life by raising the earnings of working people. The Children's Defense Fund estimates that, on average, each year of education increases a worker's hourly wages by 10% (Sherman 1994). Work by Ashenfelter and Krueger (1994) on identical twins found that each year of additional schooling raised later earnings of the more educated twin by 13%.

Moreover, as education increases in importance in the workplace, the financial returns for additional education increase.[9] The real earnings of 30-year-old American male high school graduates are 20% lower than the earnings of the comparable group 20 years ago. In 1993, according to a 1995 National Alliance of Business study, men with at least a college education earned on average 89% more than men with just a high school diploma; compared to those with only a high school education, those with at least a college degree are less likely to be unemployed, less at risk of losing their jobs, and more likely to be covered by a pension or health plan. Those with less than a high school degree saw their mean family income, in inflation-adjusted dollars, decline by 14% between 1979 and 1995. Those with a college degree or more attained an increase in their mean family income of 14.2% (Lynch 1999, 195).

In a review of the literature on school quality and earnings, David Card and Alan Krueger of Princeton University summarize the findings from 13 different studies based on eight different data sets on earnings. Card and Krueger find "a high degree of consistency across studies regarding the effect of school quality on students' subsequent earnings. The studies typically find that a 10% increase in school expenditures is associated with a 1 to 2 percent increase in annual earnings for the students later in life" (Card and Krueger 1996). In most cases, these studies control for level of education, meaning that the estimated income increase represents an increase *for a given level of schooling*. Furthermore, "increases in school resources are also associated with significantly higher educational attainment, although the range of estimates of the effect is wider. . . . The similarity of the sign and magnitude of the estimated elasticities in the literature gives us a degree of confidence that the relationship between school quality and earnings is not a chance occurrence" (Card and Krueger 1996).

Eric Hanushek, summarizing a number of other studies, documents the effects of higher school test scores on higher earnings. He writes that in the U.S. "these returns have grown dramatically over the past twenty years, particularly for a college education. During the 1990s, an average college graduate earned in excess of a 70% premium above the average high school graduate" (Hanushek 2002a).

Earlier work by Card and Krueger also demonstrated how schools of radically different quality in the segregated South produced widely divergent returns to education for black and white workers. For example, in a comparison of Southern-born blacks and whites born between 1910 and 1939 and living in Northern cities in 1960 (to control for labor market differences), Card and Kruger estimate average returns per year of schooling to have been twice as high for whites (6.0%) as for blacks (3.4%) (Card and Krueger 1992b).

Several economists have examined the value of schooling inputs by studying the relationship between school quality (measured on the basis of expenditures per student or the pupil-teacher ratio) and student outcomes (measured in terms of future earnings). This approach assumes that, since workers with higher skills tend to earn more, school quality can increase future earnings potential (holding parental education, race, and IQ constant) either by helping students to learn more per year of schooling or by increasing the number of years students stay in school. Economists Card and Krueger find that increases in school resources are positively associated with significantly higher educational attainment. Taken together, these studies document that increases in school resources can pay off for individuals and the nation.

Education spending and the quality of growth

People work in order to obtain the elements of what they perceive to be a better life. Economic development, ideally, should be helping them to meet their basic needs *and* achieve their dreams. Not only should there be enough jobs to go around, but these jobs should also pay enough to meet family needs, be reasonably secure, and provide health benefits. Moreover, workers should have the opportunity and skills they need if, for whatever reason, they want to change jobs.

A guidebook for assessing the degree to which a state is meeting this economic development goal is the *Development Report Card for the States,* published by the Corporation for Enterprise Development (CFED). The *DRC* includes over 70 data indicators to try to capture how well a state economy is doing, relative to its peers in:

- performing its job of providing residents with the opportunity for a better life (the Performance Index);
- possessing a dynamic small and large business base (the Business Vitality Index); and
- providing the foundations for future growth and opportunity (the Development Capacity Index).

One of the key findings of the 1994 *DRC* was that a state's economic performance is highly correlated to its past investments in "development capacity" (investments in human, financial, technological, and infrastructure resources).[10] Of the 11 states with the highest grades in development capacity from the 1990 report card, all but three (73%) received an A or a B in performance[11] in the 1994 report card and none received a D or an F. The reverse is true for the 10 states that received the worst grades in development capacity in the 1990 report card. All but three received a D or an F on performance in the 1994 report card, and none attained an A or a B.[12]

Given the findings from the *1994 Development Report Card for the States* showing a relationship between investments in development capacity (human resources, technology resources, financial resources, infrastructure and amenity resources) and economic performance, CFED compared the 50 states' rankings on the *DRC's* Economic Performance Index over the past 10 years with state per pupil spending on education in prior years.[13] The results of this analysis revealed a statistically significant relationship between per pupil spending and economic performance grades.[14]

The study also attempted to capture the impact of additional spending over and above the average level on a state's chances of receiving an honor grade (A or B) in economic performance.[15] The results indicate that those states spending the average amount per pupil ($4,510 in 1990-91 dollars)[16] increased their chances of receiving an A or B five years later by 1.0% with an additional $100 in spending per pupil (a 2.2% increase in per pupil spending). While not guaranteeing improved grades, this finding indicates that a spending increase of this level slightly improves a state's chances of receiving an honor grade. The results with a 10-year difference between spending and economic performance grades indicate that, at the spending mean ($3,827 in 1990-91 dollars), states can increase the probability of receiving an A or B grade by 1.3% with an additional $100 in spending per pupil (a 2.6% increase in per pupil spending). Again, these results, while not large, show a statistically significant positive relationship between education spending and economic performance grades on the *Development Report Card.*

CFED also found that, for those states below the spending mean, the same $100 per pupil spending increase led to a slightly larger increase in the probability of receiving an honor grade. This increased probability levels off at a per pupil spending level of between $4,000 and $5,000. In other words, a state spending below the national average is likely to experience increasing returns to scale, on average, for additional per pupil spending; a state spending above the national average is likely to experience quickly decreasing returns to scale, on average, for additional per pupil spending.

In addition, CFED sought to evaluate the relationship between education spending and the three sub-indices of the Economic Performance Index. Two sub-indices demonstrated a statistically significant relationship:

- *The Earnings and Job Quality Sub-Index*, which measures pay and benefits, had a positive and statistically significant relationship to education spending. Increasing per capita spending on education by $100 at the mean increased the probability of a state's receiving an A or B on this sub-index by 1.4%.

- *The Equity Sub-Index*, which measures the poverty rate and income distribution, also had a positive and statistically significant relationship to education spending. Increasing per capita spending on education by $100 at the mean increased the probability of a state's receiving an A or B on this sub-index by 1.8%.

These results confirm what one might expect, given the earlier discussion about the importance of education for economic development. First, due to high and increasing returns to education, education's greatest economic impact is in decreasing poverty and in generating a more equitable distribution of income. Second, due to these same factors, education also has a positive impact on earnings. Third, because educated workers are a critical factor in high-skill, high-performance companies, but not necessarily in all companies, it is understandable that the study did not find a statistically significant relationship between education spending and the Employment Sub-Index (the third sub-index of the Economic Performance Index). In other words, the impact of education on employment tends to vary from state to state, depending in part on each state's mix of employers.

It should be noted that, given our earlier discussion about the nature of economic development and how it encompasses more than just jobs and wages, these findings concerning the relationship between education spending and grades on the *DRC* may understate the overall impact of education spending on economic development.

The social costs of inadequate educational and workforce preparation opportunities

By increasing earnings, education can also lower social costs. For instance, unequal educational opportunities are linked to social problems, such as drug abuse, crime, and lack of access to medical care, that can put a hefty drag on the economy. According to researchers Gordon Berlin and Andrew Sum (1988),[17] there is a strong relationship between low basic skills and welfare dependency — 60% of out-of-wedlock births among 19- to 23-year-olds are to those who score in the lowest 20% on basic skills tests. Berlin and Sum estimate that raising the means-tested skills of 19- to 23-year-olds by the equivalent of one grade would increase lifetime earnings by 3.6% and reduce the likelihood of births out of wedlock by 6.5%, welfare dependency by 5.3%, and arrests by 6.2%. Similar work by the corporate Committee on Economic Development cites these disturbing statistics:

- About 82% of all Americans in prison are high school dropouts, and it costs an average of $20,000 annually to maintain each prisoner.

- Investing $4,800 per child in preschool education can reduce teenage arrests by 40%.

Researchers Barbara Wolfe and Robert Haveman, in a more recent study along these lines, sought to calculate the public and private returns on additional schooling. When they totaled both market and non-market yields, they found a full rate of return that could be as high as 14-18%. Indeed, "because few other public or private investments seem able to claim returns of this magnitude, a reallocation of resources from other uses to the education sector may be in order" (Wolfe and Haverman 2002, 119).

Economist Richard Freeman's research also points out that the social costs of crime and incarceration are so high that almost any current public intervention would pass a cost-benefit test. He calls the U.S. policy strategy to combat crime the "Great Incarceration Experiment." The U.S. spends almost 10 times as much as Western European countries on security services, arrest, incarceration, and parole, while these same European countries spend comparable amounts on subsidized employment, training, and transfer payments. (Moreover, the real pay of low-skilled workers there has not fallen as it has in the U.S.)

Approximately 2% of U.S. gross domestic product is allotted to crime control activities, and another 2% presently is lost to crimes that occur. Freeman (1996) estimates that an average of $54,000 could be invested in each of the 5 million or so men in jail, on probation, or on parole and still come out ahead if the returns are comparable to programs such as the Job Corps or the highly successful Perry Pre-School Program.[18]

Thus, where one invests really matters. Indeed, wage stagnation at the bottom of the wage scale along with increased inequality in the 1980s and 1990s were caused in part by skill-biased technological change, along with the shrinkage of unions, the failure of the minimum wage to keep up with income growth and inflation, a shift from manufacturing, and increased global competition. Simultaneously, demand for less-skilled workers fell as they were displaced by automation and import competition.[19]

Although education and training are not necessarily the source of these problems, they can be part of the solution.

CHAPTER 3

Investing in what works

In what educational programs, curriculum, technologies, skills, and infrastructure should we invest increased resources? This section looks at promising opportunities in the areas of pre-kindergarten education, primary and secondary education, and community colleges.

Why does investing in pre-K matter to economic development?

Pre-K delivers. When children start out with high-quality health and educational resources, they are more likely to become productive individuals and to contribute positively to their communities. But in addition to the personal and social payoffs, research shows that resources, ranging from prenatal care to early immunizations to appropriate stimulation and preschool programs, can offer communities a real economic return on investment. This research helps to make a clear case for long-term public investment in children whose socioeconomic situations do not allow for the same resources that middle- and upper-income children often take for granted. Especially compelling is the evidence about preschool investments from longitudinal studies tracking individuals and control groups from the early 1960s to the present.

One of the long-term benchmark studies has followed the lives of 123 low-income African American 3- and 4-year olds who participated in the Perry Preschool Project in Ypsilanti, Mich. between 1962 and 1967. Half of the children participated in a high-quality preschool program, while the other half did not attend preschool. Researchers interviewed 95% of the original participants at age 27 and found that children who participated in the high-quality preschool program encountered fewer arrests as adolescents, were less likely to repeat grades, earned higher incomes (59% higher), were more likely to own homes and second cars, reported having longer-lasting marriages, had fewer children out of wedlock, and reported less utilization of welfare and other public assistance programs.[20] Researchers have quantified the return to be $7 for every $1 invested in preschool education for participants in the Perry program.[21]

Other studies provide further evidence that early education pays off. The National Institute for Early Education Research estimates a $25,000 net return per child for universal, accessible preschool for 3- and 4-year-olds (Barnett and Hustedt 2003). A study of Chicago's Child-Parent Center for 3- and 4-year-olds asserts that, for an average investment of $7,000 per child, society can expect a return of $47,759 per child by age 21 ($26,000 of which represents additional taxes paid and taxpayer savings on remedial, support, and rehabilitative services) (Wolfe and Scrivner 2003). The Michigan Department of Education, in its press release "State Funded Preschool Program Works for Children At-Risk," reported that one-third fewer children who participated in the Michigan School Readiness Program for 4-year-olds had to repeat a grade later in their education than those who did not participate. For that factor alone, the public saves $11 million in taxes annually.[22]

In their call for increased public investment in Minnesota preschool programs, Bob Grunewald, a regional economic analyst, and Art Rolnick, senior vice president and director of research for the Federal Reserve Bank of Minneapolis, state:

> Research has shown that investment in early childhood development programs brings a real (that is, inflation adjusted) public return of 12% and a real total return, public and private, of 16%. We are unaware of any other economic development effort that has such a public return, and yet early childhood development is rarely viewed in economic development terms. (Grunewald and Rolnick 2003)

Furthermore, research shows that the economic benefits of pre-K extend beyond the personal earnings and public-dollar savings of program participants. In her essay, "Investing in the Future: Reducing Poverty Through Human Capital Investments," Lynn A. Karoly cites research that "[w]hen programs are also designed to promote human capital accumulation and economic self-sufficiency among participating parents (typically the mother), there may be parenting, educational, economic, and health benefits for those parents."[23] Parents whose children receive assistance for preschool programs are better able to seek out and maintain jobs in the workplace and to participate in the political economy. And many programs, such as Head Start, often employ and train parents of participating children as child care workers.[24]

Advocates of public investment in universal pre-K have the following suggestions. A number of major organizations and corporations have stepped forward to address deficiencies in funding and to advocate for increased support, accessibility, and quality of early child care programs. For example, the Children's Defense Fund (2001) offers a concise checklist for state and federal government, including:

- Increased funding for the Child Care and Development Block Grant by $20 billion over five years to provide help to two million additional children.
- Expanded efforts to improve compensation and training for child care providers.
- Increased support for resource and referral programs to help families find child care, to strengthen the capacity of community child care providers, and to collect data.
- New funding to improve and expand child care facilities to ensure that children are in healthy, safe, and appropriate environments.

A Bank of America/United Way initiative called Success by 6 encourages corporate partnerships with public organizations to improve access and delivery of pre-K programs. The program, launched in 1998 with a $50 million-over-five-years grant from Bank of America, seeks to reach low-income children in 350 communities throughout the United States to "ensure that children from birth through age six are given the support they need to lead healthy and successful lives."[25]

Bank of America says that it supports this effort because of compelling evidence about the importance of the experiences of young children with regard to brain growth, emotional attachment, language development, and motor skills. The bank's report, co-published with the United Way, documents the return on investment in young children ages birth to 6:

- The public saves an estimated $7.16 for every dollar originally invested in high-quality child care.
- $1 invested in childhood immunizations saves $10 in childhood illness and death from illness.
- Half of all cases of mild mental retardation are preventable. The cumulative costs to age 18 of special services are 20-30% lower if begun at birth rather than at age 6.[26]

In their essay, "Providing Universal Preschool for Four-Year-Olds," Barbara Wolfe and Scott Scrivner make a strong case for supplementing public subsidies for preschool with a system that requires parents to contribute according to their financial ability. Such a program would make pre-K universal – at a sliding-scale price that would perhaps encourage greater participation of low-income families.

Finally, the business-based Committee for Economic Development (CED) has proposed "a new national compact" between state and federal government "to make early education available to all children age 3 and over." CED's proposal, *Preschool for All: Investing in a Productive and Just Society,* claims that "[f]or too long, the United States has paid lip service to the importance of preschool opportunities that prepare children for school without undertaking the level of investment needed to turn promise into reality. For the sake of both the children and of our society, it is time to make good on the commitment to provide early learning opportunities for all."[27]

Through building greater awareness of the economic benefits of universal early childhood education and the potentially negative economic consequences of failing to make it a national and state priority, these organizations hope to convince federal and state legislators of the importance of nurturing all children. Their policy proposals offer opportunities for low-income children and families, and for the communities in which they live.[28]

Primary and secondary education

Why does increased K-12 education spending matter? We know that high-quality education is critical to the earnings of individuals and the economic health of entire communities. Yet, while agreeing that quality education is important, some would disagree that increased public investment will improve the quality of education. This position is typically based on well-publicized research findings (see below) that suggest that, in terms of student achievement, "money doesn't matter." In the section that follows, we will argue, on the contrary, that education spending is important. It can:

- *have a direct, positive impact on the business climate*, not only in terms of general measures of economic health, but also specifically in terms of creating a business climate conducive to a high-value/high-wage economy, and
- *improve the success of at-risk students,* whose contributions to the economy are critical for achieving a high-value/high-wage economy in the 21st century.

Yet, while money does matter, the way it is spent matters as well. Increased spending in priority areas needs to be coupled with reforms in accountability, greater support for innovation in the classroom, and many other changes.

Can increased education spending lead to higher student achievement? While the findings from early research on human capital and those from more recent studies on the increasing returns to education have established a clear link between human capital formation (the outcome of the education process) and economic success, these studies reveal little about the economic impact of education spending (one of the inputs in the education process). After all, the argument that education spending can have a positive impact on economic health must address the legitimate concerns about how well education dollars are spent. A body of well-publicized research has put forth the notion that there is no significant relationship between school expenditures and student performance. While a complete review of the "does money matter?" debate is beyond the scope of this paper,[29] a look at its major findings is important to help clarify this issue.

The case that money doesn't matter is built largely around the work of Eric Hanushek of the Hoover Institute at Stanford University. In a seminal article entitled, "The Economics of Schooling: Production and Efficiency in the Public Schools," Hanushek examines findings from 147 separate studies that had used "education production functions" to examine the relationship between investments in education and student performance.[30] Hanushek concludes:

> The results are startlingly consistent in finding no strong evidence that teacher-student ratios, teacher education, or teacher experience have an expected positive effect on student achievement....*There appears to be no strong or systematic relationship between school expenditures and student performance.* (Hanushek 1986, 1162; emphasis added)

In a later article, Hanushek clarifies his position: "[M]ost economists, including myself, would readily accept that differences in spending would be directly related to education provided *if schools were operating efficiently.* The previously presented evidence in Hanushek's review of past education production function studies indicates clearly, however, that assuming efficiency in spending is entirely inappropriate" (Hanushek 1993; emphasis added).

Since this important work, Hanushek has been a virtual one-man research institute, producing numerous studies with colleagues that document a wide variety of supporting and detracting conclusions on the relationships between education and a variety of benefits. These findings include weak links between spending and improved educational performance, strong connections between high test scores and national economic growth rates, a correspondence between rising education costs and slow performance improvements, the factors responsible for increasing costs, the apparent failure of redistribution to affect the performance of less-wealthy school districts or to equalize outcomes (except for black females), the strong connections between test scores and labor market success, the importance of pay for attracting and retaining women teachers, a modest effect of wage increases on teacher movement within and across districts, a powerful effect of teacher turnover on school performance, a definite correlation between teacher test scores and student performance, a positive effect of class size in lower grades and especially for minorities, weak connections between school organization and leadership variables and student performance, and a large impact of teacher quality (as opposed to teacher education or experience) on school performance.[31]

However, partly in response to Hanushek's findings and partly as a result of improvements in education research (including new statistical techniques that can account for some of the problems with the data used by Hanushek), a number of recent studies have challenged Hanushek's conclusions. In certain cases, these studies question Hanushek's finding of no relationship between education spending and student performance (see Hedges et al. 1994). In other cases, the studies demonstrate that certain kinds of education inputs, such as smaller class size (see Folger 1989), more experienced or better-trained teachers (see Ferguson 1991), or both (see Ladd and Ferguson 1998) have a significant effect on student achievement. Some of the more interesting studies are discussed below.

In a reanalysis of the data used by Hanushek, researchers Larry Hedges, Richard Laine, and Rob Greenwald (1994) suggest that the data from these previous education production function studies do not support Hanushek's conclusions. To start with, Hedges et al. question Hanushek's use of "vote counting" – i.e., giving each published study equal weight ("one vote"), regardless of the amount of data it was based on, the number of statistically significant findings it produced, or the magnitude of the significance of the findings – as a procedure for analyzing the results of past studies. Because it may fail to detect statistically significant relationships and because it is unable to give an indication of the magnitude of relationships that may exist, vote counting lacks statistical power.

To overcome these problems, Hedges et al. re-analyzed Hanushek's data using a more sophisticated synthesis method known as "meta-analysis."[32] Subjecting the 187 education production function equations used by Hanushek to this analysis, Hedges, Laine, and Greenwald produced the following conclusions:

- With the exception of teacher/pupil ratio and facilities, there are "at least some positive relations between each of the types of educational resource inputs studied and student outcome" (Hedges et al. 1994, 10). Those inputs showing a positive relationship to students outcomes included per pupil expenditures, teacher experience, teacher education, teacher salary, and administrative inputs.

- In terms of the magnitude of the impact of various resources, per pupil expenditures and teacher experience demonstrate the greatest effect on student outcomes. The impact of other inputs (teacher salary, administrative inputs, facilities, class size, etc.) is more mixed.

Although it may seem contradictory that overall per pupil expenditure has such a clearly positive impact while the effect of the inputs that make up overall spending (teacher salary, class size, etc.) is more mixed, Hedges et al. argue that: "[t]his pattern of results is consistent with the idea that resources matter, but allocation of resources to a specific area (such as reducing class size or improving facilities) may not be helpful in all situations. That is, local circumstances may determine which resource inputs are most effective" (Hedges et al. 1994, 11).

In summary, Hedges et al. assert that, "the question of whether more resources are needed to produce real improvement in our nation's schools can no longer be ignored. Relying on the data most often used to deny that resources are related to achievement, we find that money *does* matter after all" (Hedges et al. 1994, 13).

In a large-scale, four-year study conducted during the late 1980s, researchers with Tennessee's Project STAR (Student/Teacher Achievement Ratio) tested the effect of class size reductions on student achievement (Folger 1989). By making use of a controlled experiment (rather than existing data), Project STAR was able to avoid some of the limitations of previous education production function research.[33]

Initially, students in 328 kindergarten classes across 79 schools were randomly assigned to either classes whose size had been reduced by approximately one-third (small classes)[34] or to a control group (regular classes). For four years (kindergarten through grade 3), Project STAR followed this large cohort of students and tested the children's achievement levels. Students remained in the same treatment group (class size) through the duration of the study; teachers were randomly assigned to classes each year. Project STAR's researchers found that:

- in each of the four years, small-class students scored significantly higher than students in regular classes in reading and math;

- the small-class achievement advantage is found in all kinds of schools: inner city, suburban, rural, and urban. However, the small-class advantage is largest, on average, in inner-city schools as compared with other types of schools;
- the effect of small classes increases from kindergarten to first grade, but beyond first grade there is no cumulative effect.

Because reducing class size is a relatively costly intervention, John Folger and Carolyn Breda of Vanderbilt University have concluded that "even the greater class size effects gained in Project STAR do not make across-the-board class size reduction an attractive or cost-effective strategy for improving student achievement" (Folger and Breda 1989). They recommend instead targeted class size reductions combined with other proven instructional techniques for improving student achievement.

An update of the research on Tennessee schools that adopted smaller class sizes in 1985-89 found that class size appreciably affected student performance, raising math and reading scores over time. These effects showed up well into junior high, even after students returned to larger classes. Students in the smallest classes did better than their peers in regular classes, no matter which school they attended and even when these schools had teacher aides. Author Frederick Mosteller concludes: "The main finding was that a small class size in the earliest grades – kindergarten, first, second, and third – speeds learning in these years and confers lasting benefits into later grades to students with this start" (Mosteller 1995). Reducing class sizes is an extremely replicable strategy, but it hinges on spending more money.

Further support for this position that money matters (at least sometimes) comes from recent research on school reform in Austin, Texas. In 1989, an important desegregation case led to the designation of 16 elementary schools as priority sites for additional monies. Each school received $300,000 more than its normal school budget, and these funds were to be used to lower student absenteeism, raise student scores on state-mandated achievement tests, and generally equalize educational outcomes across the city.

After five years, an evaluation reported important, but mixed, results. In 14 of these schools, student attendance and achievement remained low. But in two other schools, Zavala and Ortega, student attendance was among the city's highest, and the student test scores within these minority schools had risen to the city average. In addition, at Zavala and Ortega there was no "creaming" for the most-likely-to-succeed students – children still came from the same poor neighborhoods where family incomes averaged $12,000.

What was responsible for the difference in outcomes? The 14 schools where student attendance and achievement remained low used the money to keep doing what they always had done. But Zavala and Ortega principals not only decreased the size of the average classroom, they also launched a comprehensive effort to make deeper changes in teaching, student requirements, curriculum, goals, and parent involvement. They adopted the same reading and math curricula that were used in the rest of the district with gifted and talented children. They put all special-needs children into regular classes – which worked, because the smaller class sizes made it easier to give these children the attention they needed. Also critical was providing additional training to teachers on how best to use the curriculum to meet the needs of all their students.

In addition, despite opposition from the school board, faculty and parents lobbied successfully for bringing health services directly into the school. This helped Zavala and Ortega address a range of health problems that affected attendance, including immunizations and access to health care alternatives beyond the local hospital's emergency room.

The schools also invested heavily in securing increased parental involvement. They worked together with parents on developing clear achievement goals for the school, and they recruited parent volunteers to sit on school hiring and budget committees.

The ultimate finding was that money well spent on shrinking class sizes, establishing definite and understandable goals, providing high-quality and relevant teacher training, structuring incentives, and getting parents involved can improve school performance, even in the poorest neighborhoods. Evaluators also concluded that having both parents and teachers agree that student achievement was too low and that something significant had to be done provided the leverage and energy to make other changes happen (Murnane and Levy 1996).

Other support for education spending can be found in evaluations of Wisconsin's Student Achievement Guarantee in Education (SAGE) program, which seeks to reduce the student-teacher ratio to 15 students per teacher in grades K-3. According to a report by the Center for Policy

Alternatives, "SAGE is successful because it does more than lower class size – it mandates comprehensive reform. Participating school districts are required to strengthen academic curricula, implement professional development programs and accountability measures for staff, and keep school buildings open longer hours to accommodate before- and after-school programs. Annual evaluations show that SAGE students outperform students from comparable schools" (Center for Policy Alternatives 2003, 70).[35]

Hanushek's conclusions have often been supported by evidence that, as per pupil expenditures have increased, average SAT scores have decreased. But this finding has been questioned as well. In the *Harvard Educational Review*, Brian Powell of Indiana University and Lala Carr Steelman of the University of South Carolina argue that the *number* of high school seniors taking the SAT accounts for the vast majority of the variance in state scores; specifically, more students from lower socioeconomic backgrounds are taking these tests. According to the authors, "both SAT scores and ACT scores, if properly adjusted, are linked positively to school funding" (quoted in Tabor 1996).[36] For instance, each additional $1,000 per student raises SAT scores by close to 15 points.

The give-and-take involved in this outpouring of research has led Hanushek and Princeton University economist Alan Krueger to move closer in some of their opinions. At a recent conference, Hanushek stated:

> Surely class size reductions are beneficial in specific circumstances – for specific groups of students, subject matters, and teachers….Second, class size reductions necessarily involve hiring more teachers, and teacher quality is much more important than class size in affecting student outcomes. Third, class size reduction is very expensive, and little or no consideration is given to alternative and more productive uses of those resources.

Krueger said the following:

> The effect sizes found in the STAR experiment and much of the literature are greater for minority and disadvantaged students than for other students. Although the critical effect size differs across groups with different average earnings, economic considerations suggest that resources would be optimally allocated if they were targeted toward

> those who benefit the most from smaller classes. (Mishel and Rothstein 2002)[37]

Work by the Educational Testing Service draws roughly similar conclusions. Harold Wenglinksy (1997) reports that monies spent on increased teacher-student ratios raise average achievement in mathematics for fourth graders and foster fewer problem behaviors, thus improving the environment in school.

The report *Making Money Matter: Financing America's Schools*, by the Committee on Education Finance convened by the National Research Council, recommends a closer alignment between additional funds and education goals, the development of the emerging concept of funding adequacy, a more accurate estimate of the added costs of educating children from disadvantaged backgrounds, experimentation with ways to empower schools and parents to make use of public funds, and additional evaluative research. The committee identified the following goals for education finance systems to guide such work:

- education finance systems should facilitate a substantially higher level of achievement for all students, while using resources in a cost-efficient manner;
- they should facilitate efforts to break the nexus between student background characteristics and student achievement;
- they should generate revenue in a fair and efficient manner (Ladd and Hansen 1999; Wenglinsky 1997).

Thus, school funding can make a difference in student achievement. Rather than more spending across the board, each of these later studies suggests some specific areas, such as class size or teachers' skills, in which increased educational investments can make a difference. The results of this newer research into the relationship between education spending and student performance can perhaps best be summarized in the words of Johns Hopkins education researcher Robert Slavin: "It is clear (and obvious) that increased dollars do not magically transform themselves into greater learning. *But it is just as clear (and just as obvious) that money can make a difference if spent on specific programs or other investments known to be effective*" (Slavin 1994, 99; emphasis added).

Where should we invest more? Given the level of ambiguity that persists in educational evaluation research, increased or redirected investments in education should seek to:

1. *Identify the most pressing needs and the support programs best able to meet the full scale of these needs.* These programs might include targeted class size reductions, particularly for children in the early grades and children from low-income and/or minority families, and school-based reform approaches (such as accelerated schools, the Comer School Development Program, and the "Success for All" model) that combine consistently high expectations for at-risk children with school-wide support systems to help students meet these expectations.

   Furthermore, school districts should consider replication of successful approaches to reading tutoring in elementary school grades; increased incentives for the best and more experienced teachers to teach in the worst schools; assignment of teachers to teach the subjects in which they have been well-trained; investments in staff development to help teachers (a) learn the most up-to-date information on curriculum and instruction, (b) incorporate this learning into their daily lessons, and (c) work on more closely aligning instruction with goals, standards, and grade progression.

   In fact, the academic literature on serious and sustained professional development demonstrates strong positive effects on student learning and performance. Greenwald, Hedges, and Laine (1996) even found that "there is a greater increase in student achievement for money spent on professional development than for money spent on reducing class size or raising teachers' salaries." The trick seems to be that the professional development must be fully integrated with real teaching practices in specific schools.[38] General professional development, held across a district, or episodic workshops do not seem to generate a great deal of measurable return.

2. *Work at decreasing school district financial inequities and meet specified adequacy standards.* This goal must also involve earmarking any increased resources for particular purposes and programs. Upgrading learning technologies at needy schools might be one example.

Community colleges

Community colleges play a major role in U.S. higher education. Roughly one-half of all undergraduates in postsecondary institutions in fall 1997 were enrolled in community colleges. Viewed over a full year, more for-credit undergraduates attend community colleges than attend baccalaureate-granting institutions. The non-credit courses of community colleges are growing as well, and in many of these courses non-credit students outnumber degree-seeking students. Minorities and new immigrants are overrepresented in such two-year schools.

Today's community colleges are facing a more challenging environment than in the past. As Thomas Bailey writes in "Community Colleges in the 21st Century: Challenges and Opportunities":

> Changes in pedagogic and production technology; state funding policy; the expectations of students, parents, and policy makers; demographic trends; and the growth of new types of educational institutions and providers are threatening established patterns of community college activities and potentially altering the role of colleges within the wider landscape of higher education. (Bailey 2002, 60-61)

But, he writes, "community colleges…continue to enjoy many advantages. These include low tuition, local political support, and favorable demographic and educational trends." Based on these factors, many community colleges are expanding their missions to become more comprehensive schools. But some fear that such a change in direction could detract from the traditional core function of the community college – vocational education. Especially important as well are the colleges' open admission policies, remedial education services, career advisory functions, transfer programs, and links with employers and economic development institutions.

Vocational training expert Norton Grubb of the University of California, Berkeley points out that sub-baccalaureate education has grown substantially over the last decades. Presently, about 27% of the labor force has more than a high school diploma but less than a four-year degree. This trend will likely continue, given growth rates of occupations, including many in health technology fields, marketing and sales, information technology, and others, that require more training than high school but less than a university program.

The individual benefits of a community college education. The rate of return on community college education is generally positive, but the level of effect depends on the occupational choice and graduation of the student. The average community college entrant, who never attended a four-year college and enrolls but does not complete a degree, earns 9-13% more than the average high school graduate, age 19-38, with similar high school grades and test scores. Today, relative to high school graduates, both men and women with some college earn 14-17% more. (The group with "some college" includes those with associate's degrees, those who dropped out of community colleges, individuals seeking only a certificate or credential, and university dropouts.) Those with completed associate's degrees fare better: men with associate's degrees earn 18% more than high school graduates, and women 23% more (Grubb 1999a, 3).

Generally, "more formal schooling is better than less: a baccalaureate degree is superior to an associate degree, which in turn is better than taking some coursework without completing credentials" (Grubb 1999a, 5).

Because of their low cost and lack of requirements for admission, community colleges have become the postsecondary organizations that many disadvantaged groups use to gain access to employment. Research suggests that "attending a community college confers greater advantages to blacks compared to whites, and compared to remaining a high school graduate, even though some of the differences are small and uncertain" (Grubb 1999a; Grigg 1999b). For older or displaced workers who need to upgrade their employment or seek a new occupation, the effects run from poor to good. A lot of the variation is attributable to the field of study, "with substantial positive returns to health-related credits, science and math, and trades and repair, while basic or remedial education and the humanities had negative effects. If, for example, an individual took one year's worth of health-related and technical credits, the long-run increase in earnings would be about 15%" (Grubb 1999a; Bailey 2003).

As for credential effects:

- In terms of certificate programs, men achieve higher returns with engineering, computer, and health-related certificates, but much lower returns for business and miscellaneous vocational subjects. For women, health-related certificates pay off; business certificates do not. (This is not surprising, since many of these programs are designed to prepare lower-level secretaries and data-entry clerks.)
- In terms of associate's degrees, men earn higher benefits for engineering and computer jobs. Women in health professions earn more.
- In terms of baccalaureate degrees, men and women see the highest pay-off in business, engineering/computers, health, and math/science. Returns are lower in social sciences (particularly for men) and the humanities, and lower still in education (Grubb 1999a, 1).

Not surprisingly, men earn more with technical community college degrees than those with baccalaureate degrees in education or humanities.

These differences, along with research into the high non-completion rates in community colleges, suggest the need for better guidance counseling in high schools and community colleges. Indeed, those with poor high school grades and low commitment to schooling in secondary schools are unlikely to fare well in four-year or two-year colleges. Studies also point out that those who secure jobs in their fields do better than those who do not. Other research indicates that degrees and certificates play a "signaling" role for employers that job applicants are reliable, even if the jobs do not require a particular degree or applied formal training (Grubb 1999a, 1999b).

Public benefits. It is also important to document public benefits of community colleges, not just individual benefits (i.e., increased earnings). It is these societal returns – such as an educated populace – that were behind the Carnegie Commission's recommendation in 1970 that states charge low or no tuition at their community colleges. What are these benefits?

First, community colleges offer a highly cost-effective way to obtain the first two years of a bachelor's degree. The state cost per credit hour is much lower than for four-year colleges. Thus, community colleges make colleges accessible to many low-income, minority, and adult students who would not or could not attend a four-year school. As the children of the baby boom flood higher education, states should consider expanding their community colleges to meet demand.

Second, community colleges are an essential element in states' toolbox, preparing adults for the workforce through certificates and degrees, providing lifelong learning (non-credit courses), and delivering customized training and workplace literacy, thereby upgrading on-the-job skills. Moreover, community colleges rescue many high school dropouts and prepare them for productive work. Whole sectors of the economy actually depend on the technical workers that community colleges turn out – registered nurses, health technicians, engineering/manufacturing technicians, criminal justice workers, child care workers, and so forth.[39]

New directions. Thus, community colleges are well-positioned to play an important role in bridging the educational, wage, race, and class divides in the United States. Jobs for the Future President Hilary Pennington cites these reasons:

- Community colleges offer a wide range of programs from remedial and vocational education to college transfer programs.
- They are relatively flexible and responsive.
- They are closer to the employers and their organizations.
- They are respected teaching organizations.
- They operate inside the mainstream.
- Two-year colleges are positioned to "integrate the now-separate silos of K-12 and higher education, economic development, and workforce development into a real system focused on the kinds of post-secondary education and credentials that the labor market rewards."
- Many community colleges are exploring new roles for expanding economic opportunity and creating economic development linkages.[40]

CHAPTER 4

How to invest more in people

Who will pay for these education initiatives? Given the fiscal challenges facing most states, securing funding will be difficult; yet it is not an impossible situation. Federal and state governments need to take a long-term perspective, considering the significant return on investment that good public services, including a productive education and training infrastructure, can bring. Furthermore, building a sound infrastructure and improving public services cannot happen in a climate of rock-bottom taxes; such a long-term and forward-thinking perspective will demand courageous reforms in the tax system. Sound, sizable investments in education will require taking the following steps:

- Reducing the reliance on local property taxes for financing K-12 education.
- Curbing the use of profligate business incentive programs.
- Halting the use of a variety of tax-sheltering loopholes used by corporations, which are eroding revenues generated by state corporate income taxes.
- Modernizing state (and local) revenue systems.

Reforming school finance

The current method of financing K-12 education is marred by large disparities in funding among states and local school districts. States are now playing a larger role in school finance, but the local property tax is still a critical revenue base. The range in property wealth within a state means that districts with the largest number of low-income children have the least productive property tax bases.

This financial catch gives rise to two challenges:

- Will we provide schools with the resources they need to make high-quality education real?
- Will we provide the resources to all children or only some children?

These challenges, furthermore, raise another perpective on the debate about whether education spending has an effect on student performance, and that is the impact of legal challenges to state systems for funding public education. In fact, while the question of whether money matters has attracted a great deal of interest in scholarly journals, it has also become the focus of even greater attention in the courtroom.

The landmark ruling in this type of case is *Serrano v. Priest*, in which the California State Supreme Court ruled that equal access to education required equal funding:

> Although an equal expenditure level per pupil in every district is not educationally sound or desirable because of differing educational needs, equality of educational opportunity requires that all school districts possess an equal ability in terms of revenue to provide students with substantially equal opportunities for learning. (*Serrano v. Priest*, 1977)

Since *Serrano*, many states have faced legal challenges to their systems of education finance (Fulton and Long 1993). Since 1973, 43 states have experienced such litigation (Education Writers Association 2003). While each challenge involves complex legal issues, three important trends emerge. First, courts are increasingly likely to overturn state school finance systems because of funding disparities between districts. As education finance expert Allan Odden has noted: "in the 1990s almost all the courts, when these decisions come before them, are overturning state school finance systems. The batting record in the 1970s and 1980s was about .330. In the 1990s it is about .900, so it looks like if you get a court case filed, it is very likely that the system will be overturned" (Odden 1993, 113; Education Writers Association 2003, 14-26).

Second, in those states in which the system was found to be constitutional, the courts typically based their decisions *not* on a finding that education spending disparities are unimportant, but rather on a finding that education was not a fundamental right in that particular state or on arguments for local control of education. In other words, in none of those states (whose education finance systems were found to be constitutional) did the courts imply that "money doesn't matter."

Third, court decisions in states such as Kentucky, Alabama, and New Jersey have moved beyond mere spending adequacy to require states to provide equality in the depth, breadth, and quality of educational opportunities. Typically, these cases have referred to the need to teach students the kind of problem-solving and critical thinking skills that will be demanded increasingly in the job market of the future.

Lastly, the litigation is giving rise to new efforts to define adequacy. Some call this a new paradigm for viewing and correcting school financing inequities. *Money Matters: A Reporters' Guide to School Finance* states the following:

> Educational adequacy, which emphasizes how much money is needed to reach certain outcomes, is beginning to overshadow the concern for the equitable distribution of money. In other words, how much money does it take to graduate young people who are able to actively participate on a jury in a complex legal case, for instance? Even when spending is equalized among districts in a state, is there any guarantee that the money will be directed toward greater academic achievement? (Education Writers Association 2003, 1)

This shift in direction has led to a great deal of experimentation with various models to calculate what should be spent on schools; these include the successful school model, the professional judgment model, and the evidence-based model. Each has its pros and cons, and the calculations remain more art than science. But the bottom line is that spending disparities maintain a U.S. school system in which many schools are still separate and unequal (Education Writers Association 2003).

Why business incentive programs must be reformed

Twenty-five new governors assumed office in 2003 at a time when states faced their worst budget crisis since World War II. The new governors and their returning peers are under enormous pressure to reduce state expenditures and balance budgets without raising taxes or cutting essential services. As a result, fiscal circumstances have created the opportunity and the desire for major reform of state economic development incentives.

The competition between states to recruit new companies or to retain existing ones has never been more intense. Billions are spent nationwide via a variety of tax incentives and spending programs that have fueled a new economic war among the states.

According to Professor Kenneth Thomas's book, *Competing for Capital*, America's states spend approximately $49 billion annually on state and local development. These incentives take two forms: tax incentives and non-tax incentives. Tax incentives are big, and they are growing in most states faster than on-budget expenditures for economic development. As a percent of the gross income tax on manufacturing investment in 20 states studied recently, incentives rose from 9.9% in 1990 to 29.4% in 1998.

In addition, analysts have noted that the price tag for specific projects is locked in an inflationary spiral. Using recent projects to attract large automobile plants as a proxy, the cost for landing an agreement has increased from $11,000 of public money spent per job created in 1980 for the Nissan plant in Tennessee to as much as $200,000 per job created in Alabama's Mercedes Benz project in 1993 (Schweke et al. 1994, 23). The current sweepstakes to attract a major Boeing facility encouraged Washington State to offer $3.2 billion. The result is that all locationally mobile companies, whether in manufacturing, wholesaling, retail, or other sectors, now expect an incentive as part of their standard business package.

Earlier we suggested that the aim of economic development should be to achieve a more widely shared and sustainable standard of living. Sadly, of course, economic development often does not achieve this standard. Too much money is spent on low-yield, low-road activities, which produce temporary and low-wage jobs. Too much money is squandered on the business incentives competition between states and localities. Too much of the development that is promoted and financed is not environmentally sustainable. Too much of the development launched in the name of poor or economically distressed communities does not trickle down. Most importantly, while economic development policies change, often the business incentives used to support them do not keep pace, leading to a wasteful proliferation of redundant programs.

The issue of whether to use such incentives to recruit businesses presents a fundamental dilemma for cities and states. On one hand, most economists agree that incentives are not good development policy (see Lynch 2004; Schweke et al. 1994; Schweke et al. 1996; Anderson and Wassmer 2000; Fisher and Peters 1998; and Peters and Fisher 2002). Indeed, Robert Lynch's report on *Rethinking Growth Strategies: How State and Local Services Affect Economic Development*, concluded:

> An analysis of the relevant research literature…finds little grounds to support tax cuts and incentives – especially when they occur at the expense of public investment – as the best means to expand employment and spur growth. (Lynch 2004, vii)

In using development incentives to attract businesses, governments waste scarce public dollars often without creating any net new jobs, and we subsidize the shareholders of companies for economic actions they would usually have taken anyway. Furthermore, incentives foster unfair competition because they help some firms and industries and not others. This development strategy diverts policy makers from the actions they need to take to create jobs and a better business climate. Thus, tax expenditures and grants with no accountability mechanisms, that are used for attracting business, do not typically generate as high and as reliable rate of return then spending on education.

On the other hand, incentives can make a difference in the site selection process, particularly when the choice comes down to two or three similar locations. Even if the economics are bad, political pressure makes it hard for governors and mayors to ignore the incentives sweepstakes. How could any state or locality unilaterally disarm and miss the chance of landing a significant business prospect? Likewise, how can an elected official, such as a mayor or governor, avoid responding with public dollars and policy changes when a company, which has long operated in the state, threatens to leave and accept generous incentives from another jurisdiction?

The challenge is to find ways to make their jurisdictions attractive without giving away the tax base, and to use incentives selectively and responsibly.

The need to modernize state revenue systems

Broadly speaking, states and localities tax the incomes, consumption, and real estate wealth of their citizens and the profits and property wealth of businesses engaged in economic activity within their borders. Personal income taxes, household and business property taxes, consumption taxes, and taxes on corporate profits together account for 99% of state and local tax revenues. Unfortunately, technological and economic factors are interacting with longstanding deficiencies in state and local taxing powers and policies to erode the base of these taxes.[41]

Traditionally conservative claims about taxes and economic development assert that state and local taxes discourage investment, slow economic growth, and destroy jobs. There are reasons to be skeptical about these claims, however.

Business people who make location decisions rate taxes and tax incentives much lower than other critical factors, such as labor quality, market potential, and access to raw materials.[42] Indeed, state and local taxes are a relatively small share of total business costs, and many are deductible for purposes of federal taxes. This federal offset reduces the real differences in tax burdens among states: after federal deductions, all state and local taxes paid by the average business typically represent less than 2-3% of the cost of running the average business.[43] Statistical and econometric studies also show that state and local tax cuts (and incentives) have little to no effect on job creation.

Yet, a growing number of studies document that public investments, especially in education and infrastructure, actually generate jobs. In fact, several studies that examined the effects of state and local tax increases used to finance increases in public services have discovered that such tax increases may accelerate state and local economic growth. A recently published analysis by the Federal Reserve Bank of Boston further corroborates the view that tax cuts have a small to nonexistent impact on jobs and that there is a more significant and predictable positive effect from adequate public services.[44]

Fisher and Peters (2002) state that, if we accept the rough consensus position that taxes have a modest, statistically significant effect on growth, a 30% cut in state and local taxes would generate only one new job out of the 10 jobs claimed by economic development policy makers. In other words, incentives work only about 10% of the time. Without creating more new jobs, it is difficult for these programs to generate positive fiscal impacts.[45]

Others claim that progressivity in a state's personal income tax creates problems as well. However, research undermines the argument that the business climate is harmed by high personal income tax rates. A study that looked at the relationship between progressive taxation and income growth (Chernick 1997) found that such taxation had no negative effect on income growth. A separate study by Citizens for Tax Justice (2003) discovered that, based on the cumulative effects of income, property, and sales and other state and local taxes on the average family, middle- and low-income families pay much higher shares of their income in all state and local taxes than do the very well-off.[46]

The greatest obstacle to a more positive environment for business growth and profitability is not overly burdensome taxes; it is outmoded state tax systems. Reforming these systems is one of the central development *and* fiscal challenges facing many state governments. An outmoded state tax system is bad for business and for the citizenry because it is generally and increasingly out of step with today's multinational, information-based, service economy, and new demographic trends; it establishes an uneven playing field between large and small businesses, in-state firms, and out-of-state companies; it gives rise to structural deficits in many states (revenues that do not keep pace with economic growth); it creates state revenue deficiencies at the same time that Congress is cutting federal domestic spending and devising new capped block grants; and it exacerbates fairness problems – the less affluent shoulder more of the tax load, and businesses and households that earn the same income pay significantly different taxes (as a result of tax preferences).[47]

Erosion of the corporate income tax. We see these problems of outmoded state tax systems very clearly in the recent erosion of the state corporate income tax as a key revenue base.

State corporate income and franchise taxes are among the most complex and controversial areas of public finance. Forty-six states impose these taxes, and they are increasingly under assault by multi-state corporations. In 1977, the corporate income tax accounted for about 9.5% of state revenue collected, while in 1998 the number had shrunk to 6.0%. According to David Brunori of the Urban Institute, "[S]ince 1959 the corporate income tax base has failed to keep pace with corporate profits (either worldwide or domestic). In other words, in relative terms, state governments are collecting less in corporate income taxes while corporations are earning more" (Brunori 2002, 103).

Other research shows that corporate income tax revenues decreased as a percentage of state tax revenues in the recession of the early 1990s, but they also declined in the later 1990s despite an economic boom. The effective state-local corporate tax rate averaged about 6.5% in the 1980s, but in the 1990s it declined about 40% from these levels, falling to only 3.8% by 1998 (Brunori 2002, 104).

Businesses require services and impose costs on state and local governments, and the corporate income tax is meant to pay for these benefits. It is the only avenue a state has to reach those who use public services but reside outside of the state (Brunori 2002, 106-10). Moreover, corporate income taxes are basically designed to even the playing field between labor- and capital-intensive firms, regarding property versus income taxes; treat out-of-state and in-state companies in a neutral and fair fashion; and strengthen the personal income tax, because corporate taxes prevent shareholders and owners from shielding their income in corporate holdings.

The decline in the state tax levy can be attributed to a variety of factors:

- The rise of the service sector, upon which states impose fewer taxes than they do on manufacturing, and the birth of multinational corporations, which create "nowhere" income untaxed by states, mean that existing state tax systems are not yielding the revenues required, while some other sectors carry more than their fair share.

- While services are a growing share of the economy, sales taxes are generally limited to purchases of tangible goods. Only three states tax services comprehensively, and fewer than half tax services to any significant degree (Brunori 2002, 33-41). Consequently, the percentage of state revenues derived from sales taxes are not keeping pace with the demands imposed by economic growth, and states will be forced to raise sales tax rates. Taxing one sector and not another also violates the principle of neutrality, which argues that all forms of economic activity should be subject to comparable taxation.

- The transition from a goods- to a service-dominated economy, as well as trends such as globalization, have a number of implications for the structure of state tax systems. Sales tax systems, for example, tax the transfer or sale of tangible goods based on the location of the seller. When the product transferred is a service, the location of transfer may be hard to define. Who should tax the provision of legal services provided by a law firm based in New York to a business with offices in Los Angeles, Chicago, and New Orleans? How should states treat the purchase of goods from catalog sellers or Internet retailers? In addition, state corporate tax systems use a set of rules known as apportionment formulas to determine how much income a state is entitled to tax. Until recently, most states used three equally weighted factors – property, payroll, and sales – to allocate income. Now that business assets are often intangible and sales difficult to locate, businesses can create "nowhere" income that escapes taxation in any state. As the economy becomes more sophisticated and transactions more difficult to trace, states lose the ability to tax activities that they are legitimately entitled to tax.[48]

A recent study by the Multistate Tax Commission[49] (2003) documented the implications of these changes. Corporate tax sheltering is linked to as much as $12.4 billion in lost state tax revenues, or 35% of all 2001 state corporate tax commissions. California ($1.34 billion), Illinois ($693 million), Texas ($607 million), and Pennsylvania ($582 million) were hit the hardest in absolute amounts lost. West Virginia lost the highest proportion of its collections, 57.8%.

CHAPTER 5

Attaining the prerequisites for a high-wage, high-performance economy

So far, we have sought to establish that the quality and the breadth of "human capital" matters to a modern industrial economy and that current fiscal trends threaten state and local governments' ability to invest adequately and prudently in this skill base. We must pursue actions that fit today's economy and better position creative state and local governments to win in a global economy.

In fact, this policy platform has the added advantage of meshing with current trends in national and global economics. The rules of the economic game have changed. Sweeping economic changes in the past few decades have altered the ways in which states and communities must seek to strengthen their economies and provide good jobs for their people. What seemed to work well and make sense for much of the 20th century is suddenly obsolete, pushed aside by a rush of new realities linked to the further internationalization of the U.S. economy and the introduction of information technologies into the workforce.

More U.S. goods and services are facing stiff foreign competition. If the nation is to achieve a higher and more shared standard of living, U.S. firms must compete on the basis of new, higher-quality service and production approaches that utilize new technologies and a more skilled workforce.

Economic developers call this "the high road" because it offers a path to a strong economy based on, and generating, higher-paying jobs, greater productivity, and wealth. As Trent Williams of Regional Technologies puts the matter:

> You get your gross margins up by making your goods and services more aesthetic, faster, multi-functional, more accessible, more

> precise – whatever. This requires in most cases technological development, development, improvement. There are no low-tech industries, just low-tech firms. Technology is the value-added linchpin. This is where our competitive advantage lies – not in going head-to-head on cost with low-wage challengers. Talent – both blue- and white-collar – is the most important foundation for successful high-road development. (Williams 2002)

How do we travel on this high road? The best prescription would have the following three components:

1. Develop a more seamless, well-endowed lifelong learning system.
2. Reform wasteful business incentive programs and redirect savings into education or other state priorities.
3. Create and maintain a modernized revenue base.

Developing a lifelong learning system

There is a range of possible strategies that states can pursue, from improving the quality of teaching to retraining incumbent workers, to develop a lifelong learning system. Recognizing that funds are limited and that some of these strategies may have more impact than others, we will elaborate below on a few priority recommendations for states that want to link education, workforce development, and economic development in a positive way.

Improve early childhood development. Because of the importance of education to individual and community well-being, and given demographic trends that suggest that the proportion of students at risk of educational failure will grow over the next quarter century, strategies designed to make sure all children are ready for school can be expected to have a large impact on the business climate. Options for ensuring healthy early childhood development among all children include expanding early childhood screening, upgrading developmental aspects of existing day care, and improving access to developmental day care by expanding the Head Start program. States might also consider multigeneration Head Start programs that provide parenting and literacy training to parents. To coordinate existing early childhood and education efforts, states:

- can develop an inventory of available public and private child care resources;
- create mechanisms for coordinating services at state and local levels, and establish collaborative efforts between schools and other providers;
- serve as a clearinghouse for information and programs;
- collect data on services and performance, etc.

Helping at-risk students. Another education strategy for achieving significant economic impact is investing in proven techniques or promising reform approaches that will improve the performance of low achievers and other at-risk students already in school. Such approaches might include early identification and response; new learning technologies; intensive teaching and alternative learning environments; and programs to help teenage parents stay in school.

The Alliance for Excellent Education argues in *Every Child a Graduate: A Framework for an Excellent Education for Middle and High School Students* (2003) that six million students are threatened with being left behind. The Alliance suggest four major efforts:

1. an adolescent literacy initiative to provide intensive and focused literacy and tutoring that compliments the Reading First work that helps early grades;
2. a teacher and principal quality initiative to provide incentives to educators to work in high-poverty schools, to provide mentoring for new teachers, and to provide opportunities for on-going professional development. (The Alliance suggests funding levels of a $4,000 annual tax credit for teachers and principals who agree to work in high-poverty schools and $20,000-$37,500 in grants and loan forgiveness to college students agreeing to teach in needy schools for at least four years.)
3. a college preparation initiative to expand guidance counseling to help each student pursue a viable post-secondary education career path.

4. a small learning communities initiative to establish smaller schools or schools-within-schools.

Improving the school-to-work transition. Of all the educational strategies that states can pursue, perhaps those with the most direct connection to the business climate are school-to-work initiatives. These include programs like apprenticeships, tech prep education, career academies, and school-based enterprises, all of which benefit from the active participation of employers and which are designed to ease the transition from school to work by combining classroom learning with real work experience. School-to-work initiatives are targeted at the large number of high school graduates who choose not to attend a four-year college, but who nevertheless need advanced skills and training to find jobs that will pay a decent wage. The initiatives often place greater emphasis on the diverse needs of today's students in the sense that they incorporate hands-on learning and may be better suited to students who are less comfortable in a classroom setting.

Reforming education finance with a link to restructuring and accountability. Given tight budgets in statehouses across the country, along with some legitimate concerns about how well education dollars are spent, political reality dictates that, in return for more resources, schools will be required to be more accountable for improving student performance. An editorial in *Business Week* on school funding inequities said it well: "It's understandable that taxpayers don't relish spending more general revenues on consistently bad schools. And it's true that money alone won't solve the system's woes. But a system so inequitable and so inadequate in many poverty areas must change" (*Business Week* 1990). Options to enhance accountability might include combining greater accountability standards with (1) requirements for higher minimum tax efforts by localities; (2) the creation of a financing formula that would compensate poorer school districts and those with more at-risk students; (3) the creation of an incentive fund for improved performance at the school level; (4) allowing local school tax efforts beyond the minimum that is not matched by the state; and (5) allowing for a "hold harmless" period of five years with a new financing system so that no district loses money during the first few years.

Especially important is the investment of federal dollars in the "No Child Left Behind" program. It is currently an unfunded mandate that is siphoning millions out of ordinary education and into preparations for passing required achievement tests. An October 13, 2003 article in *The Washington Post* reported that both Democratic and Republican governors are finding it impossible to comply with the law without additional federal dollars.

Financing community colleges. In a classic study, *The American Community College* (Cohen and Brawer 1996), the authors stated: "For thousands of students, the choice is not between a community college and another institution of higher institution, the choice is between a community college and nothing." Providing access to post-secondary education is part of community colleges' core mission. In the past, this prime directive has been followed through open door admissions, affordable tuition, and the provision of classes for transfer and workforce education that are geographically accessible in the college's service area (Coley 2000).

But community colleges are facing challenges in preserving access with excellence. State funding for higher education has been declining and tuition costs have risen. Simultaneously, college enrollments are growing rapidly. These changes are especially hard on rural community colleges. In some states, community colleges are partially dependent on local property taxes, and so they also suffer the effects of low-wealth tax districts. A renewed commitment is needed to:

- increase access for all low-income students by exploring changes in funding formulas, such as the percentage of costs that tuition covers; by recognizing the higher operating expenses of rural colleges; and by seeking new revenue streams that will lessen the impact of economic downturns;

- target more monies for colleges to collaborate with local industry on workforce preparation and retraining;

- invest in opportunities for community colleges to close the digital divide in central city and urban locations;

- support continuous education and noncredit education (see Katsinas et al. 2003).

Reforming business incentives. Poorly designed and profligate business incentive programs can negatively affect education and other workforce development strategies by directly undermining the local property tax base of school financing and diverting monies from state educational and training initiatives.

State policy makers should avoid the rush to match the incentive-mad offers of other states. Such development races will lead to eventual disaster – growing fiscal shortfalls, indiscriminate deal making, and political backlash. Instead, a smarter approach is to ensure that tax and non-tax incentives are integrated into larger state and local economic development policies and that their use meets the highest standards of fiscal integrity.

Economically, incentives are largely a bad idea, but they can help some states and communities attract or keep companies. Although there is still no ideal model in existence, innovative state governments should act on the following directives:[50]

- *Curb the use of wasteful tax expenditures and impose stronger performance and accountability standards on tax expenditures.* For example, policy makers should not hide revenue choices and aid to particular businesses and households in the most obscure parts of the tax code. Many mechanisms can promote accountability. Some states favor sunset review for tax incentives, while others favor periodic reporting – called tax expenditure reports – of tax provisions creating exceptions for designated groups, and periodic assessments of tax policy overall or its impacts on groups of different incomes or geographic location.

- *Develop a "certified" cost-benefit methodology.* States should consider setting a minimum standard for evaluating incentive programs and special deals. After such a model approach is developed, they should encourage all states and localities to use it when measuring net benefits and net costs per job for varied development incentives. Such a tool can be used to help evaluate recruitment projects and the economic efficiency of the business incentive package, as well as assess legislative proposals for new incentives.

- *Cooperate with other states on issues like uniformity and the runaway costs of business incentives.* For the state corporate income tax to work effectively for interstate business, uniformity is the key. The principal underlying it is that all states imposing corporate income taxes use the same or similar rules for determining how corporations are taxed. Making reforms like those proposed above can enjoy support from some of the business community. A survey by Coopers and Lybrand found that many multi-state companies would welcome state tax codes with more uniform definitions across states and that they believe that this simplification would lower their companies' compliance costs (Coopers & Lybrand 1994).

- *Consider the educational impact of any major incentive deals or policy changes.* It is important to remember that misguided economic development policies can have a direct and negative impact on education. Good Jobs First, in its recent study *Protecting Public Education From Tax Giveaways to Corporations* (2003), offered these specific recommendations: (1) improve disclosure of potential revenue effects of tax increment financing[51] and property tax abatements that could shrink school funds; (2) give local school boards authority in subsidy decisions; and (3) seek to have state government shield local school revenues from the effects of these tax-based subsidies by reimbursing school districts for any monies lost.

Creating a high-quality revenue system

Reformers on both sides of the political aisle must admit that in tax and fiscal policy, as in most areas of public life, it is difficult to combine all appropriate goals of a fair and far-sighted tax policy. The main challenge is to avoid either starving the public sector of essential revenues or burdening businesses with unnecessary taxes and complexity. There will be no real progress if liberals or conservatives deny the dangers of erring on either side.

Development-enhancing tax reform is inseparable from the "reinventing government" agenda. It is always important to get the best returns from fiscal spending by investing scarce tax resources in the highest-priority and highest-yielding public investments and making government service delivery more efficient, effective, customer-friendly, and accountable. Efforts to create a high-quality revenue system and good government go hand-in-hand. Having the revenue needed to invest in education requires better tax systems.

Although the agenda for reform is complicated and particulars will differ from state to state, an action agenda for innovative states can be summarized in a few simple recommendations.

Broaden and modernize the tax base. Old features of the tax code might irrationally penalize emerging industries. Indeed, by modernizing the tax system and avoiding traditional business-climate tax cutting or incentive schemes, states are much more likely to end up with a broader, fairer, and simpler revenue base with lower rates.[52]

Make sure that multi-state corporations pay their fair share. States should implement tax policies that ensure that multi-state corporations have state corporate income tax and sales tax liabilities similar to those faced by wholly in-state corporations. These policies include mandatory "combined reporting" (an accounting method that treats businesses comprising a parent and subsidiaries as one corporation for state corporate tax purposes) and the assertion of taxing jurisdiction over out-of-state corporations to the limits permitted by federal law. By seeking long-term changes in federal law, states can move toward taxing out-of-state corporations that make substantial sales to their residents (including resident businesses).

Conclusion

One of the principal challenges for states and localities is to find ways to promote more employment in high-value work. The evidence reviewed in this book demonstrates that high-quality education and workforce preparation, while not sufficient, is a *necessary* condition for meeting this challenge. Neither a quality school system nor a pool of skilled workers will, by itself, convince local firms to shift into high-value mode, encourage new high-value enterprises to start, or attract high-value companies from outside. Without such a school system or such workers, however, communities will have a difficult time becoming centers for high-value economic activity.

Thus, state policy makers can raise the rate of return on their economic development and education dollars. Such success requires only the political courage necessary to develop a 21st century tax base, to terminate ineffective incentive programs, and to spend available dollars on high-yield education programs. The reward will be growth, as well as equity.

Endnotes

1. See *State Budget Actions*, published annually by the National Conference of State Legislatures, Denver, Colo.

2. Education at this level provides students with many of the basic skills necessary for success in the labor market and also provides the foundation for pursuing higher education or further workforce training. While both of these aspects of education are also of critical importance to business climate, they are beyond the scope of this chapter.

3. See, for example, Schultz 1963.

4. See, for example, Greenspan 1995 and Marshall and Tucker 1992.

5. See Coffey and Polese (1995) for a discussion of the role of entrepreneurs in regional economic development.

6. See Malecki 1983 for a pioneering and classic discussion of the role of technology in regional development.

7. "Internal rate of return" refers to the discount rate that equalizes the present value of lifetime earnings associated with differing levels of education. For similar research literature examples, see Cypher and Dietz (1997) and Todaro (1997). For a more qualified view, see Easterly (2001) and Krueger and Lindahl (2001). The latter article points out that "education is both the seed and flower of economic development."

8. The education spending variable used in this study was total state and local education expenditures from own sources as a percentage of state personal income.

9. See, for example, the testimony of Lawrence F. Katz at a hearing of the Joint Economic Committee, U.S. Congress, on *Creating High-Wage Jobs in a Global Economy*, September 16, 1992. Katz suggests that increasing educational wage differentials, with the earnings of young male college graduates increasing by 30% relative to those with 12 or fewer years of schooling, are one of three primary causes for increasing wage dispersion.

10. In the 1994 *DRC*, the Development Capacity Index was made up of 24 measures, grouped into four sub-indices: human resources (including high school graduation and college attainment), technological resources (including Ph.D. scientists and engineers in the workforce and patents issued), financial resources (including commercial bank deposits and venture capital investments), and infrastructure and amenity resources (including highway quality measurements and energy costs).

11. When this study was conducted, the Performance Index was a benchmark that evaluated the extent to which a state's economy provides its citizens with

economic benefits and opportunities for growth. The Performance Index consists of 11 individual measures gathered into three sub-indices, the Employment Sub-Index, the Earnings and Job Quality Sub-Index, and the Equity Sub-Index.

12. While the data that support this finding are not strong enough to suggest, in any sense, that investment in development capacity "causes" high economic performance (the relationship may be the reverse), it demonstrates a strong relationship.

13. The decision to use per pupil spending as the education spending variable was based on two assumptions: (1) that those states with high average spending on education are likely to receive high Economic Performance grades, and (2) that increasing average spending per pupil will likely result in higher Economic Performance grades. Further, the study chose average spending rather than spending change because spending change: (1) assumes that every percentage increase in education spending is equally good, (2) overcompensates for those with the lowest levels of spending, and (3) places at a disadvantage those states already close to an optimum spending level.

14. In conducting this study, CFED performed two sets of analysis – one with a lag of five years between spending figures and economic performance grades, and one with a lag of 10 years, all over an 11-year period ending in 1993. In using this lag between education spending and economic performance grades, the assumption was that the returns from investments in education would not appear immediately but rather would emerge in the long run as students completed school and entered the workforce. Indeed, it is possible that even a 10-year lag is still too short of a period in which to capture the full benefits from investments in education.

15. In obtaining these results, CFED conducted a *probit*, which attempts to capture qualitative responses both on per pupil spending on education and on whether or not the state received an honor grade (A or B) that year, for all the 50 states as a group over 11 years.

16. Because the measures used to create the *Development Report Card* grades are not adjusted for cost of living, and because the study lacked an appropriate purchaser price index for education inputs (cost of books, cost of teachers, etc.) in each state, the education spending figures were not adjusted for cost-of-living differences among states.

17. For earlier work on this subject, see also Haveman and Wolfe (1984).

18. I am not proposing that all these funds could be shifted. But the EU/U.S. numbers give the reader a sense of priorities and opportunity costs, relative to the two policies.

19. The literature in this area is vast. Good places to begin are Sheldon Danziger and Peter Gottschalk (1995), *American Unequal*; Frank Levy (1998), *The New Dollars and Dreams: American Incomes and Economic Change*; Richard Freeman (editor), *Working Under Different Rules* (1994); and Fishlow and Parker (editors), *Growing Apart* (1999).

20. An overview of the Perry Preschool Project results is available at http://

www.highscope.org/Research /PerryProject/perrymain.htm. See also the National Institute for Early Education Research home page for a list of "fast facts," resources, papers, project reviews, and other publications related to preschool benefits at http://nieer.org/resources. Finally, Barnett and Hustedt (2003) offer an easy-to-read overview.

21. Return on investment is based on, among other factors, the taxes paid on additional earnings and the tax dollars saved by not having to pay for repeated classes, remedial learning programs, public assistance, and so on.

22. The January 23, 2003 press release is available at http://www.state.mi.us/mde/off/boards/news/news012302.pdf.

23. Karoly's essay appears in Danziger and Haveman (2001).

24. For a comprehensive review of the literature available on the benefits (personal, social, and economic) of high-quality preschool education, see Kathleen Cotton and Nancy Faires Conklin's "Research on Early Childhood Education" on the SIRS database at http://www.nwrel.org/scpd/sirs/3/topsyn3.html.

25. See http://national.unitedway.org/sb6/ for more information.

26. See Bank of America/United Way Success by 6, *National Movement, Measurable Impact.*

27. See the executive summary and complete policy statement of *Preschool for All: Investing in a Productive and Just Society* at the CED web site, www.ced.org.

28. Many additional resources define and analyze the economic benefits of preschool. A few include Barnett and Escobar (1987); Consortium for Longitudinal Studies (1983); Irvine (1982); Stalling and Stipek (1986); and Brown (1985).

29. For more on this debate, see Hanushek (1986); Murnane (1991); Ferguson (1991); and Ladd and Hansen (1999).

30. An adaptation from the world of economics, education production functions are perhaps the most commonly used technique for examining the relationship between investments in education and student performance. Just as economists use standard production functions to study the relationship between the inputs (land, labor, capital) and products or outputs produced by industry, education production functions serve similarly to study the relationship between education inputs (class size, length of school day, teacher experience, teacher pay) and outputs (typically measured in terms of standardized test scores).

31. See the following National Bureau of Economic Research working papers: Hanushek and Kim (1995); Hanushek and Rivkin (1996); Hanushek, Kain, and Rivkin (1998); Hanushek and Somers (1999); Hanushek, Kain, and Rivkin (1999); Hanushek (2002a); and Hanushek (2002b).

32. Meta-analysis is a more sophisticated synthesis method that permits the researcher to perform both combined significance tests and effect magnitude analyses. For more, see Hedges et al. (1994).

33. For example, most of the studies reviewed by Hanushek use cross-sectional data rather than longitudinal data. Longitudinal data allow a more accurate assessment of the cumulative effect of inputs over time. Also, most of the production function studies used by Hanushek are too simplistic to address effectively issues of causation.

34. Project STAR provided for an average reduction in class size from 23 to 15 children.

35. For more background, see the University of Wisconsin at Milwaukee website (School of Education).

36. For details, see Powell and Steelman (1996). The authors point out that past studies have not corrected the data on SAT and ACT scores according to the proportion of students who take the tests. They find that typically states with higher scores have fewer and better students taking the test.

37. Interestingly, Hanushek's early research supported the position that the variation in educational outcomes was so large within schools that good education seemed to be mainly a classroom phenomenon, not a school- or district-wide one. For an overview of this important literature, see Edward Pauly, *The Classroom Crucible: What Really Works, What Doesn't, and Why.*

38. Also worth reading on this topic is Wenglinsky (2000). An outstanding literature review of this topic was authored by Ulrich C. Reitzug, University of North Carolina (Janurary 2002) in *School Reform: The Evidence* (edited by Alex Molnar).

39. For more background on these issues, see Stephen Katsinaa, King Alexander, and Ronald Opp, *Preserving Access With Excellence: Financing for Rural Community Colleges,* Rural Community College Initiative, MDC, 2003. Also helpful are Tony Zeiss (editor), *Economic Development: A Viewpoint from Business* (1989) and Tony Zeiss, *Developing the World's Best Workforce: An Agenda for America's Schools* (1997).

40. These points are drawn from a series of speeches by Pennington: "Better and Faster: Accelerating Advancement in School and Work" (February 2002); "Taming the Hydrant: The Impact of Technology on Education" (January 2001); "From Best Practices to Large Scale Change: Address to the League for Innovation in the Community College" (March 2002); and "Connecting the Dots: The Leadership Imperative for the New Century" (October 2001). These are available at www.jff.org.

41. Support for this view can be found in National Conference of State Legislatures and National Governors' Association (1991) and Brunori (1998). For a more "philosophic" rationale, see Stephen Holmes and Cass Sustein, *The Costs of Rights: Why Liberty Depends on Taxes* (1999), and Liam Murphey and Thomas Nagel, *The Myth of Ownership: Taxes and Justice* (2002). Finally, Roger Vaughan's *Taxation and Economic Development* (1979) is still the best on this subject.

42. There are countless such studies that document the importance of skills and the lesser importance of incentives. A recent one is Dennis Rondinelli and William Burpitt, *Do Government Incentives Attract and Retain International Investment? A*

Study of Foreign-Owned Firms in North Carolina (Kenan Institute of Private Enterprise, Kenan-Flagler Business School, University of North Carolina at Chapel Hill, 1999). For a classic, more comprehensive look at the topic, consult Michael Kieschnick, *Taxes and Growth: Business Incentives and Economic Development* (1981). Also very helpful is the textbook, *Industrial Location: Principles, Practice and Policy,* by Harrington and Warf (1995).

43. For background literature, Lynch (2004), Schweke et al. (1996); Fisher and Ditsler (2003); and Wayslenko (1997). Other reasons exist for the relatively insignificant impact of taxes on economic development. Tax theory and experience indicate that taxes are capitalized in land values; a high tax jurisdiction will have lower land values, reflecting the additional costs of taxation. In this way, higher tax burdens are partly offset by lower costs of acquiring property. Thus, the real cost differentials between jurisdictions are minimized.

44. See Tannenwald (1996). It is very important to make valid comparisons when appraising tax burdens. Many of the typical approaches are misleading and present a false picture. Bad examples include: (1) failing to look at the total burden of all state and local taxes; (2) focusing on one high tax measure and not seeing if it is offset by lower taxes in other areas; (3) focusing on tax rates and not how the base is calculated (which of course can radically change the effects of the rates); (4) using ineffective proxies for tax burden, such as tax effort measures; and (5) punishing wealthier states by choosing the wrong indicator, etc. Also consult: Fisher and Ditsler (2003); Anderson and Wassner (2000) ; Fisher and Peters (1998); Peters and Fisher (2003).

45. See Peters and Fisher (2003) and Fisher and Ditsler (2003).

46. Typically, critics of progressivity focus on one aspect of a state's tax system while ignoring others. California, for example, has a progressive income tax, but it also has high sales and excise taxes that increase the burden on lower-income families. Critics often note that executives, who make site location decisions, are subject to the highest tax rates under a progressive system. Since personal income taxes are deductible for federal tax purposes, the after-tax effect of a progressive rate structure is minimized.

47. The discussion of these six outcomes is based strongly on National Conference of State Legislatures/National Governors' Association (1991).

48. Shrewd corporations and their advisors find ways to create "nowhere income" that is not subject to tax. Aggressive tax planning allow companies to "shelter" their income by using intercompany transactions of the choice of pass-through entity, such as a limited liability company to carry out their multi-state business.

49. The Multistate Tax Commission was created in 1967, and 45 states now participate in its effort to create increased uniformity in state tax systems and protect state revenue bases.

50. However, good places to start can be found in Puritan et al. (November 2003), *The Policy Shift to Good Jobs,* and Schweke et al. (1994; 1996).

51. One of the most widely used state and local economic development programs is tax increment financing. TIFs have been developed primarily as a means to finance public investments and infrastructure improvements needed for economic development in specific areas, usually blighted areas. The TIF program largely freezes the assessed valuation of all property parcels in a designated area (the TIF district) for a specific period of years. Property taxes levied on this frozen tax base continue to accrue to local taxing bodies, but taxes derived from the increases in assessed values (the tax increment) resulting from new development are used to pay for the infrastructure needs and development expenditures in the TIF district. Unfortunately, TIFs are being used in areas that are not really blighted in order to attract companies.

52. For more detail on these reform principles, see National Conference of State Legislatures/National Governors' Association (1991); Snell (1994); and Brunori (2002).

Bibliography

Alliance for Excellent Education. (nd.) *Every Child a Graduate: A Framework for an Excellent Education: Executive Summary.* http://www.all4ed.org

American Federation of Teachers. 2000. *Doing What Works: Improving Big City School Districts.* Washington, D.C.: AFT.

American Youth Policy Forum. 2000. *Raising the Bar: The Promise of Standards-Based Education Reform.* Forum Brief, February 25.

Anderson, J., and Wassmer, R. 2000. *Bidding for Business: The Efficacy of Local Economic Development Incentives in a Metropolitan Area.* Kalamazoo, Mich.: Institute for Employment Research.

Anderson, L., et al. 2002. *A Decade of Public Charter Schools.* Palo Alto, Calif.: SRI International.

Ashenfelter, O., and Krueger, A. 1994. "Estimates of the Economic Returns to Schooling From a Sample of Twins." *American Economic Review,* December.

Bahl, R. 1995. "Taxation and Economic Development in Ohio: A Blueprint for the Future." *State Tax Notes,* March 13.

Bailey, T. 2002. "Community Colleges in the 21st Century: Challenges and Opportunities." In *The Knowledge Economy and Post Secondary Education: Report of Workshop.* Washington, D.C.: National Academy of Sciences.

Bailey, T. 2003. "Community Colleges in the 21st Century: Challenges and Opportunities." *Community College Research Center Brief,* January.

Ballot Initiative Strategy Center. 2003. *History of the Initiative and Referenda Process.* http://www.ballot.org/resources/history.html

Barnett, W. and Escobar, C. 1987. "The Economics of Early Intervention: A Review." *Review of Educational Research,* 57.

Barnett, W., and Hustedt, J. 2003. "Preschool: The Most Important Grade." *Educational Leadership,* April.

Bartel, A. 1994. "Productivity Gains From the Implementation of Employee Training Programs." *Industrial Relations,* 4.

Bartik, T. 1991. *Who Benefits From State and Local Economic Development Policies?* Kalamazoo, Mich.: Upjohn Institute for Employment Research.

Bartik, T. 1996. *Growing State Economies: How Taxes and Public Services Affect Private-Sector Performance.* Washington, D.C.: Economic Policy Institute.

Bender, E., and Bartelds, K. (nd.) *Statewide Education Initiatives and Referendum.* Washington, D.C.: Ballot Initiative Strategy Center.

Bergman, T. (nd.) "Training: The Case for Increased Investment." *Employment Relations Today* 21(4).

Berlin, G., and Sum, A. 1988. *Toward a More Perfect Union: Basic Skills, Poor Families, and Our Economic Future.* Ford Foundation Project on Social Welfare and the American Future. New York, N.Y.: Ford Foundation.

Berliner, D. 2001. "Averages That Hide the True Extremes." *Washington Post,* January 28.

Borman, G., and Hewes, G. (nd.) *The Long-Term Effects and Cost-Effectiveness of Success for All.* Unpublished paper.

Bowles, S., and Gintis, H. 2001. *Schooling in Capitalist America Revisited.* Unpublished paper.

Brizius, J. 1994. *Deciding for Investment: Getting Returns on Tax Dollars.* Washington, D.C.: National Academy for the Public Administration.

Broder, D. 2001. *Democracy Derailed: Initiative Campaigns and the Power of Money.* New York, N.Y.: Harvest Books.

Brown, B. 1985. "Head Start: How Research Changed Public Policy." *Young Children* 40: 9-13.

Brunori, D. 2001. *State Tax Policy: A Political Perspective.* Washington, D.C.: Urban Institute.

Bulkley, K., and Fisler, K. 2002. "A Decade of Charter Schools: From Theory to Practice." *CPRE Policy Briefs.* Graduate School of Education, University of Pennsylvania.

Business Week. 1990. "School Reform and Some Basic Arithmetic."1990. *Business Week,* June 4.

Card, D., and Krueger, A. 1992a. "Does School Quality Matter? Returns to Education and the Characteristics of Public Schools in the United States." *Journal of Political Economy,* February.

Card, D., and Krueger, A. 1992b. "School Quality and Black-White Relative Earnings: A Direct Assessment." *Quarterly Journal of Economics,* February.

Card, D. and Krueger, A. 1996. *School Quality and Earnings: A Survey.* Working Paper No. 5708. Cambridge, Mass.: National Bureau of Economic Research.

Carnavale, A., and Reich, K. 2002. *A Piece of the Puzzle: How Education Is Making Welfare Reform Work in the States.* Princeton, N.J.: Educational Testing Service.

Center for Education Reform. *Answers to Frequently Asked Questions, About School Choice.* http//edreform.com/

Center for Education Research, Analysis, and Innovation. 2002. *1999-2000 Results of the Student Achievement Guarantee in Education (SAGE) Program Evaluation.* Milwaukee, Wis.: School of Education, University of Wisconsin-Milwaukee.

Center for Policy Alternatives. 2003a. "Education: SAGE." *2003 Policy Summary.* Washington, D.C.: CPA.

Center for Policy Alternatives 2003b. "Initiative Campaign Funding Disclosure." *2003 Policy Summary.* Washington, D.C.: CPA.

Chernick, Howard. 1997. "Tax Progressivity and State Economic Progress." In *Economic Development Quarterly* 11(3).

Children's Defense Fund. 2001. *State Developments in Child Care, Early Education, and School-Age Care 2001.* Washington, D.C.: CDF.

Citizens for Tax Justice. 1996. *Who Pays: A Distributional Analysis of the Tax System in All 50 States.* http://www.ctj.org.html

Coffey, J., and Polese, T. 1995. "Local Development: Conceptual Bases and Policy Implications" *Regional Studies* 19.

Cohen, A., and Brawer, F. 1996. *The American Community College: Third Edition.* San Francisco, Calif.: Jossey-Bass.

Coley, R. 2000. *The American Community College Turns 100.* Princeton, N.J.: Educational Testing Service.

Colvin, R. 2003. "What's Wrong With our Schools?" *State Legislatures,* September.

Committee for Economic Development. 2001. *Measuring What Matters: Using Assessment and Accountability to Improve Student Learning.* Washington, D.C.: CED.

Consortium for Longitudinal Studies. 1983. *As the Twig Is Bent . . . Lasting Effects of Preschool Programs.* Hillsdale, N.J.: Lawrence Erlbaum Associates.

Coopers & Lybrand, Multistate Tax Services. 1994. "State and Local Taxes: The Burden Grows: A Report on Coopers & Lybrand's 1993 Business Surveys." *State Tax Notes,* February 21.

Corporation for Enterprise Development. 1986-2003. *The Development Report Card for the States.* Washington, D.C.: CFED.

Cotton, K., and Conklin, N. 1989. *Research on Early Childhood Education. School Improvement Research Series.* Topical Synthesis No. 3. http://www.nwrel.org/scpd/sirs/3/topsyn3.html

Cronin, T. 1989. *Direct Democracy: The Politics of Initiative, Referenda, and Recall.* Cambridge, Mass.: Harvard University Press.

Cypher, J., and Dietz, J. 1997. *The Process of Economic Development.* New York, N.Y.: Routledge.

Danziger, S., and Gottschalk, P. 1995. *America Unequal.* New York, N.Y.: Harvard University and Russell Sage Foundation.

Danziger, S., and Haveman, R., eds. 2001. *Understanding Poverty.* Cambridge, Mass.: Harvard University Press.

Denison, E. 1985. *Trends in American Economic Growth 1929-1982.* Washington, D.C.: Brookings Institution.

Duscha, S., and Graves, W. 1999. *State Financed and Customized Training Programs.* Submitted to U.S. Department of Labor, Office of Policy and Research.

Easterly, W. 1997. *The Elusive Quest for Growth: Economists' Adventures and Misadventures in the Tropics.* Cambridge, Mass.: MIT Press.

Economic Policy Institute. 2002. "Small Class Size Still Matters as Deficits and Tougher Standards Loom." Press Release, June 27. Washington, D.C.: EPI.

Education Writers Association. 2003. *Money Matters: A Reporter's Guide to School Finance.* Washington, D.C.: EWA.

Federal Reserve Bank of Boston. 1997. "Proceedings of a Symposium on the Effects of State and Local Public Policies on Economic Development." *New England Economic Review,* March/April.

Ferguson, R. 1991. "Paying for Public Education: New Evidence on How and Why Money Matters." *Harvard Journal of Legislation,* Summer.

Ferguson, R. 2002. *What Doesn't Meet the Eye: Understanding and Addressing Racial Disparities in High-Achieving Suburban Schools.* Cambridge, Mass.: Kennedy School of Government. Unpublished manuscript.

Fisher, P., and Ditsler, E. 2003. *Taxes and State Economic Growth: Myths and Realities.* Ames: Iowa Policy Project.

Fisher, P., and Peters, A. 1998. *Industrial Incentives: Competition Among American States and Cities.* Kalamazoo, Mich.: Institute for Employment Research.

Fishlow, A., and Parker, K., eds. 1999. *Growing Apart: The Causes and Consequences of Global Wage Inequality.* New York, N.Y.: Council on Foreign Relations.

Folger, J., ed. 1989. "Project STAR and Class Size Policy." *Peabody Journal of Education* 67 (Fall).

Freeman, R. 1994. "How Labor Fares in Advanced Economies" and "Lessons for the United States." In Freeman, R., ed., *Working Under Different Rules.*

Freeman, R. 1996. "Why Do So Many Young American Men Commit Crimes and What Might We Do About It?" *Journal of Economic Perspectives,* Winter.

Gale, W., et al. 2003. *An Economic Perspective on Urban Education.* Conference Report No. 15. Washington, D.C.: Brookings Institution.

Gannett News Service Special Report. (nd.) *Race, Poverty, and the Achievement Gap.* http://gannettonline.com/

Golonka, S., and Matus-Grossman. 2001. *Opening Doors: Expanding Educational Opportunities for Low-Income Workers.* New York, N.Y.: MDRC.

Gordon, D., ed. 2003. *A Nation Reformed? American Education 20 Years After "A Nation at Risk."* Cambridge, Mass.: Harvard Education Press.

Great Schools Issue Paper: School Size. http://weac.org/GreatSchools/Issuepapers/schoolsize.htm

Greenspan, A. 1995. "The Creation of Economic Value in the 21st Century." *The Region.* Minneapolis, Minn.: Federal Reserve Bank of Minneapolis, December.

Grubb, N. 1999a. "The Economic Benefits of Pre-Baccalaureate Education: Results From State and Local Studies." *Community College Research Center Brief,* September.

Grubb, N. 1999b. "The Economic Benefits of Sub-Baccalaureate Education: Results From National Studies." *Community College Research Center Brief,* June.

Grunewald, R., and Rolnick, A. 2003. "Early Childhood Development = Economic Development." Editorial. *Fedgazett,* March.

Holmes, S., and Sustein, C. 1999. *The Costs of Rights: Why Liberty Depends on Taxes.* New York, N.Y.: W. W. Norton.

Hanushek, E. 1986. "The Economics of Schooling: Production and Efficiency in the Public Schools." *Journal of Economic Literature,* September.

Hanushek, E. 1993. "Can Equity Be Separated From Efficiency in School Finance Debates?" In E.P. Hoffman, ed., *Essays on the Economics of Education.* Kalamazoo, Mich.: W.E. Upjohn Institute for Employment Research, pp.48-49.

Hanushek, E. 1999. *Schooling, Inequality, and the Impact of Government.* Working Paper No. 7450. Cambridge, Mass.: National Bureau of Economic Research.

Hanushek, E. 2002a. *The Long Run Importance of School Quality.* Working Paper No. 9071. Cambridge, Mass.: National Bureau of Economic Research. .

Hanushek, E. 2002b. *The Failure of Input-Based Schooling Policies.* Working Paper No. 9040. Cambridge, Mass.: National Bureau of Economic Research.

Hanushek, E., et al. 1994. *Making Schools Work: Improving Performance and Controlling Costs.* Washington, D.C.: Brookings Institution.

Hanushek, E., et al. 1999. *Do Higher Salaries Buy Better Teachers?* Working Paper No. 7082. Cambridge, Mass.: National Bureau of Economic Research.

Hanushek, E., and Kim, Dongwook 1995. *Schooling, Labor Force Quality, and Economic Growth.* Working Paper No. 5399. Cambridge, Mass.. National Bureau of Economic Research.

Hanushek, E., and Rivkin, S. 1996. *Understanding the 20th Century Growth in Student Spending.* Working Paper No. 5547. Cambridge, Mass.: National Bureau of Economic Research.

Harrington, J., and Warf, B. 1995. *Industrial Location: Principles, Practice and Policy.* New York, N.Y.: Routledge Books.

Harris, D., et al. 2003. "Education and the Economy: How Schools Matter." Paper commissioned for special issue of the *Peabody Journal of Education*, revisiting *A Nation at Risk,* May 16.

Haveman, R., and Wolfe, B. 1984. "Schooling and Economic Well-Being: The Role of Non-Market Effects." *Journal of Human Resources* 19.

Hedges, L., Laine, R., and Greenwald, R. 1994. "Does Money Matter? A Meta-Analysis of Studies of the Effects of Differential School Inputs on Student Outcomes." *Educational Researcher* 23 (April).

High/Scope Education Research Foundation. (nd.) *Significant Benefits: The High/Scope Perry Preschool Project.* http://www.highscope.org/Research/PerryProject/perrymain.htm

Hoffman, E., ed. 1993. *Essays on the Economics of Education.* Kalamazoo, Mich.: W.E. Upjohn Institute for Employment Research.

Holt, M. 2002. "It's Time to Start the Slow School Movement." *Phi Delta Kappan.*

Holzer, H. 1996. *What Employers Want: Job Prospects for Less-Educated Workers.* New York, N.Y.: Russell Sage Foundation.

Holzer, H., et al. 1993. "Are Training Subsidies for Firms Effective? The Michigan Experience." *Industrial and Labor Relations Review* 46.

Hungerford, T., and Wassmer, R. 2003. *K-12 Education in the U.S. Economy: Its Impact on Economic Development, Earnings, and Housing Values.* Unpublished manuscript.

Initiative and Referendum Institute. (nd.) Fact Sheet No. 2. www.iandrinstitute.org

Institute for Women's Policy Research 2002. "Job Training and Education Fight Poverty." *Fact Sheet.* Washington, D.C.: IWPR, April (revised).

Irvine, D. 1982. *Evaluation of the New York State Experimental Prekindergarten Program.* Albany, N.Y.: New York State Department of Education.

Jacobson, S. and Seltzer. (nd.) *New Roles for Community Colleges: Expanding Economic Opportunity.* Boston, Mass.: Jobs for the Future.

Kahlenberg, R. 2002. *The Problem of Taking Private School Vouchers to Scale: The Next Issue in Voucher Wars.* New York, N.Y.: Century Foundation.

Karoly, L. 2001. "Investing in People: Reducing Poverty Through Human Capital Investments. In S. Danziger and R. Haveman, eds., *Understanding Poverty,* Cambridge, Mass.: Harvard University Press.

Katsinas, S., et al. 2003. *Preserving Access With Excellence: Financing for Community Colleges.* RCCI Policy Paper. Chapel Hill, N.C.: MDC.

Katz, L.F. 1992. Testimony before the Joint Economic Committee of the Congress of the United States, hearing on *Creating High-Wage Jobs in a Global Economy,* September 16. Washington, D.C.: U.S. Government Printing Office.

Kentucky Institute for Education Research. 2000. *2000 Review of Research on the Kentucky Education Reform Act.* http://www.kier.org/2000Research.html

Kieschnick, M. 1981. *Taxes and Growth.* Washington, D.C.: Council of State Planning Agencies.

Kochan, T., and Osterman, P. 1991. *Human Resource Development and Utilization: Is There Too Little in the U.S.?* MIT Sloan School of Management. Unpublished manuscript.

Kodrzycki, Y. 2000. "New England's Educational Advantage: Past Successes and Future Prospects." *New England Economic Review,* January/February.

Kodrzycki, Y. 2002. "Education in the 21st Century: Meeting the Challenges of a Changing World." *New England Economic Review,* Fourth Quarter.

Krueger, A. 2002. *Economic Considerations and Class Size.* Working Paper No. 8875. Cambridge, Mass.: National Bureau of Economic Research.

Krueger, A., and Lindahl, M. 2001. "Education for Growth: Why and for Whom?" *Journal of Economic Literature,* December.

Krueger, A., and Zhu, P. (nd.) *Another Look at the New York City School Voucher Experiment.* Unpublished manuscript.

Ladd, H. 2002. *Market-Based Reforms in Urban Education.* Washington, D.C.: Economic Policy Institute.

Ladd, H., and Ferguson, R. 1995. "Additional Evidence on How and Why Money Matters: A Production Function Analysis of Alabama Schools." In H.F. Ladd, ed., *Holding Schools Accountable: Performance-Based Reform in Education.* Washington, D.C.: Brookings Institution Press.

Ladd, H., and Hansen, J. 1999. *Making Money Matter: Financing America's Schools.* Washington, D.C.: National Academy of Sciences.

Levy, F. 1998. *The New Dollars and Dreams: American Incomes and Economic Change.* New York, N.Y.: Russell Sage.

Lynch, L. 1992. "Private Sector Training and the Earnings of Young Workers." *American Economic Review* 82.

Lynch, L. 1999. "What Can We Do? Remedies for Reducing Inequality." In A. Fishlow and K. Parker, eds., *Growing Apart: The Causes and Consequences of Global Wage Inequality.* New York, N.Y.: Council on Foreign Relations.

Lynch, R. 2004. *Rethinking Growth Strategies: How State and Local Taxes and Services Affect Economic Development.* Washington, D.C.: Economic Policy Institute.

Malecki, E.J. 1983. "Technology and Regional Development: A Survey." *International Regional Science Review* 8.

Marshall, R., and Tucker, M. 1992. *Thinking for a Living: Education and the Wealth of Nations.* New York, N.Y.: Basic Books.

MDC Inc. 1996. *The State of the South 1996.* Chapel Hill, N.C.: MDC.

MDC Inc. 2003. *Revitalizing Rural Economies: Lessons From the Community College Initiative.* Chapel Hill, N.C.: Rural Community College Initiative.

Meier, D. 1995. *The Power of Their Ideas: Lessons for America From a Small School in Harlem.* Boston, Mass.: Beacon Press.

Meier, D., et al. 2000. *Will Standards Save Public Education?* Boston, Mass.: Beacon Press.

Minnesota Department of Employment and Economic Development. 2004. "Business Location Factors: What Determines Where?" *Minnesota Economic Trends,* January.

Miron, G., and Horn, J. 2002. *Evaluation of Connecticut Charter Schools and the Charter School Initiative.* Kalamazoo, Mich.: Evaluation Center, Western Michigan University.

Miron, G., and Nelson, C. 2001. *Student Academic Achievement in Charter Schools: What We Know and Why We Know So Little.* Kalamazoo, Mich.: Evaluation Center, Western Michigan University.

Miron, G., and Nelson, C. 2002. "What's Public About Charter Schools?" *Education Week,* May 15.

Mishel, L., and Rothstein, R., eds. 2003. *The Class Size Debate.* Washington, D.C.: Economic Policy Institute.

Molnar, A., ed. 2002. *School Reform Proposals: The Research Evidence.* Tempe: Arizona State University, College of Education, Division of Educational Leadership and Policy Studies.

Moore, M. 2002. "Texas Charter Schools: Do They Measure Up?" Brief Analysis: No. 403. National Center for Policy Analysis.

Mosteller, F. 1995. "The Tennessee Study of Class Size." In F. Mosteller, ed., *The Early School Grades*. Washington, D.C.: American Academy of Arts and Sciences.

Multistate Tax Commission. 2003. *Study: Corporate Tax Sheltering Linked to as Much as $12.4 Billion in Lost State Tax Revenues.* Press Release, July 15.

Murnane, R. 1991. Interpreting the Evidence on 'Does Money Matter.' *Harvard Journal on Legislation*, 28, 423.

Murane, R., and Levy, F. 1996a. *Teaching the New Basic Skills.* New York, N.Y.: Free Press.

Murnane, R., and Levy, F. 1996b. "Why Money Matters Sometimes." *Education Week,* September 11.

Murphy, L., and Nagel, T. 2002. *The Myth of Ownership: Taxes and Justice.* New York, N.Y.: Oxford University Press.

Nathan, Joe. 1998. "Charters and Choice." *The American Prospect,* November-December .

National Alliance of Business. 1995. "The 8.6% Payoff: Education, Training Boost Productivity." *Workforce Economics* 1. Washington, D.C.: NAB.

National Center on Education and the Economy. 2002. *America's Choice School Design: A Research-Based Model.* Washington, D.C.: NCEE and the Consortium for Policy Research in Education.

National Conference of State Legislatures. 1995a. *Early Childhood Care and Educators: An Investment That Works.* Denver, Colo.: NCSL.

National Conference of State Legislatures. 1995b. *Fundamentals of Sound State Budgeting Practices.* Denver, Colo.: NCSL.

National Conference of State Legislatures. Annual. *State Budget Actions.* Denver, Colo.: NCSL.

National Conference of State Legislatures and National Governors' Association. 1993. *Financing State Government in the 1990s.* Washington, D.C.: NCSL/NGA.

National Education Association. 1995. *How Education Spending Matters to Economic Growth.* Washington, D.C.: NEA.

National Education Association. 2003. *Class Size.* Washington, D.C.: NEA. http://www.nea.org/classsize/

National Institute for Early Education Research. (nd.) *Fast Facts: Economic Benefits of Quality Preschool Education for America's 3- and 4-Year Olds.* http://nieer.org/resources/facts/

Oregon Business Plan White Paper. (nd.) *Building High Performance K-12 Education.* Salem, Ore.: Oregon Benchmarks.

Owen, Chuck. 2002. "Community College Benefits Local Economy." *LMT Business Journal,* June 24.

Pauly, Edward. 1991. *The Classroom Crucible: What Really Works, What Doesn't, and Why?* New York, N.Y.: Basic Books.

Paxcarella, E. 1999. "New Studies Track Community College Effects on Students." *Community College Journal,* June/July.

Pennington, H. 2002. *From Best Practices to Large Scale Change: Address to the League for Innovation in Community College.* Boston, Mass.: Jobs for the Future.

Peters, A., and Fisher, P. 2002. *State Enterprise Zone Programs: How Have They Worked?* Kalamazoo, Mich.: W.E. Upjohn Institute for Employment Research.

Peterson, P., ed. 2003. *Our Schools and Our Future: Are We Still At Risk?* Palo Alto, Calif.: Stanford University, Hoover Institute.

Pfleger, K. 2003. "States Play High Stakes Game to Try to Outstate Rivals for 7E7 Plant." *Seattle Post,* October 21.

Pomp, R. 1993. *Corporate Tax Data and the Right to Know.* Albany, N.Y.: Fiscal Policy Institute.

Powell, B., and Steelman, L. 1996. "Bewitched, Bothered, and Bewildering: The Use and Misuse of State SAT and ACT Scores." *Harvard Educational Review,* Spring.

Psacharopoulos, G. 1981. "Returns to Education: An Updated International Comparison." *Comparative Education Review* 17, pp. 321-341, as cited in Sturm, R., 1993, *How Do Education and Training Affect a Country's Economic Performance? A Literature Survey,* Santa Monica, Calif.: Rand Institute on Education and Training.

Puriefoy, W. 2003. "Education: America's No. 1 Priority." *State Legislatures,* September.

Purinton, Anna, et al. 2003. *The Policy Shift to Good Jobs: Cities, States, and Counties Attaching Job Quality Standards to Development Subsidies.* Washington, D.C.: Good Jobs First.

Ranii, D. 1996. "Pay Gap Linked to Education." *Raleigh News and Observer,* March 31.

Ravitch, D. 1997. *Student Performance Today.* Policy Brief No. 23. Washington, D.C.: Brookings Institution.

Research and Policy Committee of the Committee for Economic Development. 2002. *Preschool for All: Investing In a Productive and Just Society.* http://www.ced.org/docs/report/report_preschool.pdf

Rosenbaum, J. 1999. "Unrealistic Plans and Misdirected Efforts: Are Community Colleges Getting the Right Message to High School Students?" *Community College Research Center Brief,* October.

Rosenfeld, S. 1999. "Community College/Cluster Connections." *Community College Research Center Brief,* December.

Ross, D. 2002. "Reforming School Reform." *Blueprint.* Washington, D.C.: Progressive Policy Institute.

Rothstein, R. 1998a. "Charter Conundrum" *The American Prospect,* July-August.

Rothstein, R. 1998b. "When States Spend More." *The American Prospect,* January-February.

Rothstein, R. 1999. "Blaming Teachers." *The American Prospect,* December 6.

Rothstein, R. 2000. "Charter Schools in Action: Renewing Public Education." *The American Prospect,* July 31.

Sawhill, I., ed. 2003. *One Percent for the Kids: New Policies, Brighter Futures for America's Children.* Washington, D.C.: Brookings Institution Press.

Schmidt, D. 1989. *Citizen Lawmakers.* Philadelphia, Pa.: Temple University Press.

Schouten, F., and Bivins, L. 2002. "Dirty Little Secrets in Education: 10-month Investigation Reveals Inequities in Educational System." *Gannett News Service.*

Schultz, T.W. 1963. *The Economic Value of Education.* New York, N.Y.: Columbia University Press.

Schweke, W., Rist, C., and Dabson, B. 1994. *Bidding for Business: Are Cities and States Selling Themselves Short?* Washington, D.C.: Corporation for Enterprise Development.

Schweke, W., Rist, C., and Dabson, B. 1996. *Improving Your Business Climate.* Washington, D.C.: Corporation for Enterprise Development.

Sherman, A. 1994. *Wasting America's Future: The Children's Defense Fund Report on the Costs of Child Poverty.* Boston, Mass.: Beacon Press.

Slavin, R. 1994. "After the Victory: Making Funding Equity Make A Difference." *Theory Into Practice,* Spring.

Smith, S. 2003. "Putting the Financial Squeeze on Schools" *State Legislatures,* September.

Snell, R. 1994. "Our Outmoded Tax System." *State Legislatures,* August.

Snipes, J., et al. 2002. *Case Studies of How Urban School Systems Improve Student Achievement.* New York, N.Y.: MDRC.

Stallings, J., and Stipek, D. 1986. "Research on Early Childhood and Elementary School Teaching Programs." In M.C. Wittrock, ed., *Handbook of Research on Training*, 3rd ed. New York, N.Y.: Macmillan.

Sturm, R. 1993. *How Do Education and Training Affect a Country's Economic Performance? A Literature Survey.* Santa Monica, Calif.: Rand Institute on Education and Training.

Success for All. (nd.) *Frequently Asked Questions: Research on Success.* Baltimore, Md.: Success for All Foundation. http://www.successforall.net

Sum, A., et al. 2002. *The Twin Challenges of Mediocrity and Inequality: Literacy in the U.S. From an International Perspective.* Princeton, N.J.: Educational Testing Service.

Tabor, M. 1996. "SAT Ranks for the States Are Disputed: Study Links Scores to School Financing." *New York Times,* March 27.

Tannenwald, R. 1996). "State Business Tax Climate: How Should It Be Measured and How Important Is It?" *New England Economic Review,* January/February.

Thomas, K. 2000. *Competing for Capital: Europe and North America in a Global Era.* Washington, D.C.: Georgetown University Press.

Todaro, M. 1997. *Economic Development,* Sixth Ed. Reading, Mass.: Addison-Welsey.

U.S. Census Bureau. 2001. *School Enrollment – Social and Economic Characteristics of Students, October 2000.* http://www.census.gov/population/www/socdemo/school.html

Vaughan, R. 1979. *State Taxation and Economic Development.* Washington, D.C.: Council of State Planning Agencies.

Wasylenko, M. 1986. *The Effect of Business Employment on Employment Growth: Final Report of the Minnesota Tax Study Commission.* Vol. 2, Staff Papers.

Wenglinsky, H. 1997. *When Money Matters: How Educational Expenditures Improve Student Performance and How They Don't.* Princeton, N.J.: Educational Testing Service.

Wenglinsky, H. 2000. *How Teaching Matters: Bringing the Classroom Back Into Discussions of Teacher Quality.* Princeton, N.J.: Educational Testing Service.

Wenglinsky, H. 2003. *The Effect of Class Size on Achievement: What the Research Says."* Policy Information Memorandum. http;//www.ets.org;research/pic/memorandum.html

Wolfe, B., and Haveman, R. 2002. "Social and Nonmarket Benefits From Education in an Advanced Economy." In *Proceedings From an Economic Conference on Education in the 21st Century.* http://www.bos.frb.org/economic/conf/conf47/index.htm

Wolfe, B., and Scrivner, S. 2003. "Providing Universal Preschool for Four-Year-Olds." In I. Sawhill, ed., *One Percent for the Kids: New Policies, Brighter Futures for America's Children.* Washington, D.C.: Brookings Institution Press.

Zeis, T. 1989. *Economic Development: The View From Business.* Washington, D.C.: American Association of Community Colleges.

Zeis, T. 1997. *Developing the World's Best Workforce: An Agenda for America's Community Colleges.* Washington, D.C.: American Association of Community Colleges.

Titles of particular interest to educators from the Economic Policy Institute

Reports are available at the EPI website, www.epinet.org.

Class and Schools: Using Social, Economic, and Educational Reform to Close the Black–White Achievement Gap

Richard Rothstein

The wide and persistent achievement gap between black and white students is a key measure of the nation's failure to achieve true equality. As federal and state officials pursue tougher accountability and other reforms at the school level, they are neglecting an area that is vital to narrowing the achievement gap: social class differences that affect learning. *Class and Schools* — co-published by the Economic Policy Institute and Teachers College, Columbia University — shows that social class differences in health care quality and access, nutrition, childrearing styles, housing quality and stability, parental occupation and aspirations, and even exposure to environmental toxins play a significant part in how well children learn and ultimately succeed.

Teacher Quality: Understanding the Effectiveness of Teacher Attributes

Jennifer King Rice

Teacher quality is the single most important school-related factor influencing student success. In this study Jennifer King Rice examines the body of research to draw conclusions about which attributes make teachers most effective, with a focus on aspects of teacher quality that can be translated into policy recommendations and incorporated into teaching practice.

Inequality at the Starting Gate: Social Background Differences in Achievement as Children Begin School
Valerie E. Lee and David T. Burkam
Inequality at the Starting Gate examines the learning gap between rich and poor children when they enter kindergarten. This study, by two education experts from the University of Michigan, analyzes U.S. Education Department data on 16,000 kindergartners nationwide, showing the direct link between student achievement gaps and socioeconomic status. The report finds that impoverished children lag behind their peers in reading and math skills even before they start school. The book also reveals how a lack of resources and opportunities can cause lasting academic damage to some children, underscoring the need for earlier and more comprehensive efforts to prepare children to succeed in school.

Market-Based Reforms in Urban Education
Helen F. Ladd
In the debate over reforming urban education, the issues surrounding market-based approaches — charter schools, vouchers, public school choice — are complex. This EPI book examines the extensive but disparate evidence to help determine whether these reforms promote the public interest and translate well into the provision of compulsory education.

The Class Size Debate
Lawrence Mishel and Richard Rothstein, editors; Alan B. Krueger, Eric A. Hanushek, and Jennifer King Rice, contributors
Two eminent economists — Professors Krueger and Hanushek — debate the merits of smaller class size and the research methods used to gauge the efficacy of this education reform measure. Professor Rice synthesizes their arguments and highlights the points of agreement in their different perspectives.

School Vouchers: Examining the Evidence
Martin Carnoy
Does a voucher threat make schools try harder? A recent Florida study of this education reform approach said yes, but three analyses that replicate its methods show there's no basis for that claim.

Where's the Payoff? The Gap Between Black Academic Progress and Economic Gains
Jared Bernstein
Blacks have made substantial progress toward closing educational gaps, yet their wages and employment opportunities continue to lag. A review of the evidence suggests that blacks are more likely than whites to be affected by adverse labor market trends, and they have the added burden of labor market discrimination.

Can Public Schools Learn From Private Schools? Case Studies in the Public & Private Sectors
Richard Rothstein, Martin Carnoy, and Luis Benveniste
Rothstein, Carnoy, and Benveniste report on case studies of eight public and eight private schools, which they conducted to determine whether there are any identifiable and transferable private school practices that public schools can adopt in order to improve student outcomes. The evidence from interviews with teachers, administrators, and parents yields a surprising answer, one that should inform our policy debates about school choice, vouchers, public school funding, and other education issues.

School Choice: Examining the Evidence
Edith Rasell & Richard Rothstein, editors
Opinions about school choice have been formed largely on the basis of theoretical assertions that it offers the answer for the problems of public education. But researchers studying actual programs find that choice of schools neither raises student achievement nor enhances equality of opportunity, and may exacerbate racial segregation and socioeconomic stratification.

The State of Working America 2002-03

Lawrence Mishel, Jared Bernstein, Heather Boushey

The State of Working America, prepared biennially since 1988 by the Economic Policy Institute, sums up the problems and challenges facing American workers. The authors present a wide variety of data on family incomes, taxes, wages, unemployment, wealth, and poverty - data that enable them to closely examine the impact of the economy on the living standards of the American people. This latest edition will be welcomed by journalists, government leaders, researchers, policy makers, professors, and others eager for a comprehensive portrait of the economic well-being of the nation.

Where's the Money Going? Changes in the Level and Composition of Education Spending, 1991-96

Richard Rothstein

A detailed analysis of spending by representative school districts shows that real per pupil spending in the U.S. grew by only 0.7% from 1991 to 1996, and a growing share of the new money has been earmarked for special education. As a result, in some school districts spending on regular education has actually decreased in the 1990s. This study updates the 1995 EPI report, *Where's the Money Gone?,* which examines school spending for the years 1967-91.

Risky Business:
Private Management of Public Schools

Craig E. Richards, Rima Shore, & Max B. Sawicky

Doubts about government efficiency have embraced public education, which in today's global environment is viewed as a critical matter for the nation's youth. *Risky Business* examines one idea for education reform that has attracted the attention of local officials: hiring business firms to manage public schools or public school systems.

Shortchanging Education: How U.S. Spending on Grades K-12 Lags Behind Other Industrial Nations

Edith Rasell & Lawrence Mishel

This 1990 briefing paper contrasts U.S. education spending with that of its industrial competitors.

About EPI

The Economic Policy Institute was founded in 1986 to widen the debate about policies to achieve healthy economic growth, prosperity, and opportunity.

In the United States today, inequality in wealth, wages, and income remains historically high. Expanding global competition, changes in the nature of work, and rapid technological advances are altering economic reality. Yet many of our policies, attitudes, and institutions are based on assumptions that no longer reflect real world conditions.

With the support of leaders from labor, business, and the foundation world, the Institute has sponsored research and public discussion of a wide variety of topics: trade and fiscal policies; trends in wages, incomes, and prices; education; the causes of the productivity slowdown; labor market problems; rural and urban policies; inflation; state-level economic development strategies; comparative international economic performance; and studies of the overall health of the U.S. manufacturing sector and of specific key industries.

The Institute works with a growing network of innovative economists and other social science researchers in universities and research centers in the U.S. and abroad who are willing to go beyond the conventional wisdom in considering strategies for public policy.

Founding scholars of the Institute include Jeff Faux, distinguished fellow and former president of EPI; Lester Thurow, Sloan School of Management, MIT; Ray Marshall, former U.S. secretary of labor, professor at the LBJ School of Public Affairs, University of Texas; Barry Bluestone, Northeastern University; Robert Reich, former U.S. secretary of labor; and Robert Kuttner, author, editor of *The American Prospect,* and columnist for *Business Week* and the Washington Post Writers Group.

For additional information about the Institute, contact EPI at 1660 L Street NW, Suite 1200, Washington, DC 20036, (202) 775-8810, or visit www.epinet.org.